S c r i p t i
H i t c h c o c k

Scripting
Hitchcock

PSYCHO, THE BIRDS, AND MARNIE

Walter Raubicheck & Walter Srebnick

UNIVERSITY OF ILLINOIS PRESS *Urbana, Chicago, and Springfield*

Library of Congress Cataloging-in-Publication Data
Raubicheck, Walter, 1950–
Scripting Hitchcock : Psycho, The Birds, and Marnie /
Walter Raubicheck and Walter Srebnick.
p. cm.
Includes bibliographical references and index.
ISBN 978-0-252-03648-4 (cloth) — ISBN 978-0-252-07824-8 (pbk.)
1. Hitchcock, Alfred, 1899–1980—Criticism and
interpretation. 2. Motion picture plays, American—History
and criticism. 3. Motion picture authorship. 4. Film
adaptations—History and criticism. 5. Screenwriters—
United States. 6. Psycho (Motion picture : 1960) 7. Birds
(Motion picture) 8. Marnie (Motion picture) I. Srebnick,
Walter. II. Title.
PN1998.3.H58R38   2011
791.4302'33092—dc22   2011006826

To the memory of

Joseph Stefano,

Evan Hunter, and

Jay Presson Allen

Contents

Acknowledgments

A number of people played indispensable roles in helping us bring this book into print. Our colleague Steven Goldleaf read several drafts of the manuscript and offered valuable suggestions about the scope and direction of our project. Amy Gilman Srebnick provided a historian's keen judgment, an editor's eye, photographic expertise, and a supportive presence that kept us on track at every stage of our work. Sidney Gottlieb read the manuscript at a late stage, and his knowledge and judgment helped make our argument more coherent. Each of these people deserves our special thanks.

During our research trips to Los Angeles, Marilyn Stefano was a warm, generous, and hospitable source of support, especially during the times we interviewed her late husband, Joseph Stefano. Barbara Hall and the staff of the Herrick Library of Motion Pictures graciously assisted us with the invaluable screenplays and letters that formed the research basis of this study. Several of Hitchcock's other screenwriters provided important insights into the director's working methods: Arthur Laurents, Samuel Taylor, John Michael Hayes, and Ernest Lehman. Hilton Green, who worked closely with Hitchcock on *Psycho* and *Marnie,* shared with us crucial information about how certain scenes in these films were prepared and photographed. And Dorothy Herrmann shared her memories of Hitchcock's collaboration with her father, Bernard Herrmann.

Other individuals provided essential research and sources, such as Victoria Johnson and Richard Fabrizio; others shared ideas or offered encouragement, such as Janet Cutler, Richard Allen, and James Naremore. Still others gave us helpful material, such as Dina Hunter, the widow of Evan Hunter, and Brooke Allen, the daughter of Jay Presson Allen; or shared memories, such as Janet Leigh and Tippi Hedren; or offered contacts and connections, such as Lorna Champagne, Ruth Prigozy, John Lepre, Donna Mills, and Larry Gilman.

Last of all, we would like to thank our editor, Joan Catapano, for her assistance, patience, and professionalism.

Preface

From 1960 to 1964, Alfred Hitchcock directed three films that have a special stature among his work. Two of them—*Psycho* (1960) and *The Birds* (1963)—are the most-watched movies of his career and have had a profound effect on American popular culture and the history of film, and the third, *Marnie* (1964), has grown in critical and popular estimation until it is now considered one of the essential films in the Hitchcock canon. Some four decades later, the authors of this book met and came to know the screenwriters of these films—Joseph Stefano, Evan Hunter, and Jay Presson Allen—and after numerous interviews and personal and social interactions we decided to write a book on their collaboration with Hitchcock. We believe that the story of how each screenplay came into being will provide fresh insights into these films and their meaning.

Our interest in writing a book on the creation of Hitchcock's screenplays had its genesis more than two decades ago, in June 1986, at a conference we coordinated at Pace University that focused upon five other Hitchcock films: *Rope* (1948), *Rear Window* (1954), *The Trouble with Harry* (1955), *The Man Who Knew Too Much* (1956), and *Vertigo* (1958). These five films had been kept out of circulation for twenty-five years and only became available again for viewing in 1983–84. The conference was held at what was perhaps the height of "theory" as a critical force in cinema studies and in academia in general. Our collection, *Hitchcock's Rereleased Films: From* Rope *to* Vertigo, was the outgrowth of that conference, and its essays largely followed a theoretical direction.[1] One section of the book, however, transcribed a talk by Samuel Taylor, the writer who completed the screenplay of *Vertigo,* and the Q-and-A session that followed it. Taylor was one of two screenwriters we had invited to the conference and whom we got to know well. The other was John Michael Hayes, who wrote *Rear Window, To Catch a Thief, The Trouble with Harry,* and *The Man Who Knew Too Much.* While Hayes had to cancel at the last minute for personal reasons, numerous discussions with Taylor and Hayes over the next several years about their collaboration with Hitchcock left an indelible impression on us and suggested a further way to look at these films.

We quickly realized that the screenwriters offered a valuable way to understand the artistic decisions and collaboration that determined the direction of the narratives, the characters, and the meaning of these films. The writers had had extensive discussions with the director in preproduction, during which they developed together the storyline for the films and worked out their underlying motifs. It was they who then wrote all the dialogue as the various drafts of the screenplay were developed. After Hitchcock, they were the most important element in the films' production. We did not realize at the time that these two writers and the kind of information and insights they contributed foreshadowed a developing academic discourse on the circumstances of film production.

In 1999 we were organizers and coordinators of New York University's Hitchcock Centennial, at which Hitchcock's collaborators, particularly his screenwriters, played an important role. Unfortunately, Taylor, Hayes, and Ernest Lehman, whom we also invited, were unable to attend. However, there were important panels and interviews with a number of writers, particularly with Joseph Stefano, Evan Hunter, and Jay Presson Allen, that convinced us that the three films they wrote, which were produced in succession—*Psycho* (1960), *The Birds* (1963), and *Marnie* (1964)—offered a singular opportunity for studying the dynamics of their production and artistry and formed an artistic unit, or "triptych," within Hitchcock's work. The close relationships we subsequently developed with these three writers led to the idea for this book.

We found the three writers to be thoughtful and articulate about their work with Hitchcock. We began to understand how the process of collaboration in creating the screenplay was essential to understanding the final form of the film and how it came to be. The weeks the writers spent meeting face-to-face with Hitchcock as they discussed the story and the characters, and then the weeks and months they spent writing and rewriting the script, were crucial determinants of the film's artistic quality. So the next several years were devoted to our finding out as much information as we could from these writers and from our research into what they wrote.

Our interviews, discussions, and social interactions with the three of them gave us insights into Hitchcock's mind and art. (Further discussions with Taylor, Hayes, Ernest Lehman, and Arthur Laurents, who wrote *Rope,* added to our understanding of how these and other Hitchcock films were created.) Numerous trips to the Herrick Library of Motion Picture Arts in

Los Angeles to study Hitchcock's papers, production materials, and the many drafts of the screenplays of the three films helped us understand how they had evolved. We developed a new way to look at Hitchcock, and this focus on collaboration became the direction of this book.

This intensive study of Hitchcock's collaboration with these three writers led us to see the director's artistic goals and techniques in a new light. None of the writers claimed sole authorship of the scripts. They all agreed that Hitchcock could have justifiably taken a screenwriting credit for himself: he chose the sources, helped to conceptualize the plots and many of the scenes, guided the writers toward construction of characters and sequences that would work visually, and supervised the revisions of their first drafts as he envisioned the transfer of the words on paper to the screen. As the writers explained Hitchcock's contributions to the screenplays to us, our awareness of his cinematic aesthetic deepened, and we came to understand his approach to the narrative and visual coherence of each scene in the films. The writers attested to the fact that they learned more about filmmaking from Hitchcock than from any other director and that no other director they worked with had his mastery of every facet of the medium. They were always aware that they were working on a "Hitchcock picture," so our study of his writers inevitably became a study of Hitchcock as well.

A number of studies have treated the creation and production of these films individually, such as Stephen Rebello's *Alfred Hitchcock and the Making of* Psycho (1990) and Tony Lee Moral's *Alfred Hitchcock and the Making of* Marnie (2002). These two works consider the source material and the screenplays, but do so in passing and essentially as background to a more detailed study of the production of these films. Others have explored Hitchcock's working methods over the course of his career, including his extensive collaborations, such as Dan Aulier's *Hitchcock's Notebooks* (1999), Bill Krohn's *Hitchcock at Work* (2000), and Will Schmenner and Corinne Granof's *Casting a Shadow: Creating the Alfred Hitchcock Film* (2007). They each contain some material on the screenplays, but they do not study their extensive process of evolution. Still other works have chronicled the director's collaboration and interaction with an individual screenwriter, such as Steven De Rosa's *Writing with Hitchcock: The Collaboration of Alfred Hitchcock and John Michael Hayes* (1999), which, while it focuses exclusively on the Hitchcock/Hayes films, offers valuable insights into how Hitchcock worked closely with a writer on drafting a script.[2]

While our book has benefitted from these works, what we have written differs from these and other works on Hitchcock in several distinct ways. Looking in detail at the original source, we examine not only what was retained for the film, but what was changed as the narrative and characters were reconceived. Then we chronicle the intensive process of script development as the new conception evolved through the interaction of director and writer into a final shooting script, taking note of what was dropped from the screenplay by the director and how this affected the final film. Lastly, we examine the writer's most important and signature contribution, the dialogue and directions of the final script, and the role these play in determining the film's meaning and artistic success.

We regard the three films Hitchcock released between 1960 and 1964 as a triptych: a project that began with *Psycho,* continued through *The Birds,* and concluded with *Marnie*—three films that have related themes and echoes of one another, even though other projects were considered and abandoned during this period. Drawing upon our extensive interviews and interactions with the writers and our study of the screenplays, we will examine the evolution of the screenplays and the narrative, character, and textual connections among them. And, when relevant, we will look at the role of contemporary cultural and social issues (such as what we call "therapeutic" culture) in the creation of the screenplay, as film theory has asserted that culture is another "writer" of a film.

All three writers were quite open about their memories and supportive of our project, and we were able to follow up initial interviews with later ones. While some of what they told us reiterated what they had said elsewhere, there was much that was fresh and new, especially about the process of collaboration. They were all somewhat amused about the amount of scholarly and critical interest their work had generated, especially since they insisted that none of the scholarly or theoretical concerns that had been proposed to them over the last three decades had ever been part of their discussions with Hitchcock during the original project. But they were all pleased to have the attention that they felt that they as individual artists, and that film writers in general, had been previously denied. They further believed that Hitchcock stood out among the directors they had worked with in deserving the serious attention he had received. He also gave them continuous encouragement and professional respect during the period they worked with him, and the experience remained one of the highlights of their writing careers.

Interestingly, none of them found him to be the repressed, malevolent figure of Donald Spoto's *The Dark Side of Genius* (1983).[3] He seemed more a perplexing combination of intimacy and remoteness, of sociability and loneliness, and of enthusiasm and detachment who appeared to know exactly what he wanted from them but insisted that the actual scriptwriting was their "job" and not his. Each was adamant about how much they had liked him, even if there were moments of tension in the working relationship. Perhaps most impressive was their recognition that they had collaborated with one of the few acknowledged masters of the cinema. They were, however, always aware that they were creating a commercial product: they expected to earn their salaries, learn something, gain an excellent line on their resumes, and move on.

Joseph Stefano impressed us as a warm, humorous, patient, and gentle man who was exceedingly generous with his time; he entertained us at his house in Los Angeles several times and gave us signed copies of the *Psycho* shooting script, of which he was deeply proud. Of the three, he seemed the most reflective about his collaboration with Hitchcock and the director's work in general. He was aware of the extent of Hitchcock scholarship, some of which he was familiar with. When he and Hitchcock were working on *Psycho,* they considered the film largely as a piece of good entertainment. He insisted that they were both surprised by its success, the initial controversy about its violence, and the intellectual discussion it generated. He acknowledged that with time the film had grown on him and that he understood how it had moved American cinema in a new direction, as David Thomson is the most recent to argue.[4]

Stefano described himself as having been South Philadelphia–street smart and self-educated when he worked with Hitchcock; his formal education had not even included a high-school diploma. But he had broad intellectual interests and was extremely well informed and well read. At the time he wrote *Psycho,* he had a natural dramatic and theatrical sense as a writer, but his actual experience in the theater was confined to performing in musicals, or what he called being "a chorus boy," and having written popular songs, industrial shows, and one television play. He had come out to Hollywood the year before his work on *Psycho* almost on a whim and had immediate success with his *Playhouse 90* script and with the screenplay for *The Black Orchid* (1958), directed by Martin Ritt. He was extremely gratified to be working with Hitchcock so early in his film career and saw it as a career-defining experience. He went on to write numerous films and TV dramas over the next forty years and to co-create the classic TV series *The Outer Limits,* which debuted in 1964. But he always considered his collaboration with Hitchcock one of the artistic peaks of his working and creative life and was extremely gratified at the choice of the screenplay of *Psycho* by the Director's Guild in 2002 as one of the hundred greatest in the history of film.

Evan Hunter turned out to be a wry, somewhat cynical commentator on the process of writing *The Birds* and on the critical attention it has received; he seemed disappointed with the finished film but genuinely pleased that it ranked in the top ten thrillers of all time, as judged by the American Film Institute. Of the three films in our triptych, it is clear that he had adapted the original source material, the short story by Daphne du Maurier, more extensively than the other two writers did with the sources of their respective films. Hunter grew up in New York as a self-described "artistic child" whose ethnic urban family recognized and nurtured his gifts. Abandoning visual art for writing in early adulthood, he became an accomplished author who could rapidly turn out well-received fiction in several genres: adventure, mystery, and science fiction, not to mention excellent topical novels such as *The Blackboard Jungle* (1954) and *Strangers When We Meet* (1958), for which he wrote the screenplay when it was made into a film in 1960 by Richard Quine. Of the three writers, he was the most well known and successful at the time he worked with the director, and he commanded the highest salary. Open and direct, he had an outgoing, available manner, possessed an ironic sense of humor, exuded charm, and was generous with his time and help. He believed that his more than fifty 87th Precinct police-procedural novels (a genre he virtually created under the pen name Ed McBain) were his greatest achievements as a writer—and more defining of who he was than *The Birds,* although they were never sufficiently acknowledged by American critics. During the time he was working with Hitchcock, he took umbrage at commentators who described him as a "screenwriter" and insisted that he was a novelist who happened to have written some screenplays. Although he was fired from *Marnie* by Hitchcock, he maintained a special fondness for the director and for years harbored the dream of working with him again. He published a memoir of their collaboration, *Me and Hitch,* in 1997.[5]

By contrast to Stefano and Hunter, Jay Presson Allen brought a no-nonsense, facts-only attitude to our interviews: she never cared for the film she wrote for Hitchcock, or the Winston Graham novel it was based upon, but was always grateful for what she learned from the director and how he introduced her to screenwriting. She was the most difficult of the three to interview and the least in awe of the scholarly interest that Hitchcock had generated. She was especially dismissive of feminist and theoretical approaches to film, which she insisted was a popular, commercial art form whose claims to intellectual high seriousness had been blown out of proportion by academics. She also had no problem writing the "rape" scene that she felt Hunter was naïve in rejecting.

Allen believed that the praise for *Marnie,* and for her work on it in particular, was undeserved, and that the film was partially a testament to her inexperience. She could be blunt in her opinions of the limitations of some of the people she had worked with on the film. (Whenever she strayed from her own relationship to Hitchcock to give us her opinions of the performers in *Marnie* or other writers and filmmakers, she asked us to turn our tape recorder off.) Of the three writers, she had the least experience in film when she worked with Hitchcock, but she went on to become the most accomplished screenwriter, with the films *The Prime of Miss Jean Brodie* (1969), *Cabaret* (1972), *Prince of the City* (1981), and *Deathtrap* (1982) to her credit. The daughter of a Texas family that owned a department store, she possessed the most upper-class background of the three and brought this to play in some of her characterizations of social class in the film. She had a special attachment to the Hitchcocks and maintained a close friendship with them until their deaths.

Sadly, all three writers died in 2005 and 2006. Their comments to us represent their final, retrospective thoughts on their work with Hitchcock, so they are even more valuable than we had expected them to be when the writers first met with us.

This book is a study of how Allen, Hunter, and Stefano worked with Hitchcock—from the selection and adaptation of the source to the finished shooting script of each film. We begin by defining the triptych represented by the three films in the broader context of screenwriting and narrative in Hitchcock; we then explore the source of each film and how it was adapted and tailored to fit the director's cinematic conception; next we examine how the screenplays evolved as the writers reworked them and the director edited them to bring them as close as possible to his conception of what he wanted on the screen, a conception shaped in part by the collaborative process; and lastly we examine the ways in which the narratives and characters of each film were constructed and developed, with special attention to the role of dialogue and stage directions in the final script.

These were three outstanding films produced at the height of Hitchcock's career, a time when he stood in a singular relationship to the film industry commercially and artistically. At this moment he was perhaps the most popular filmmaker in America, and these three movies were drawing more attention at the box office and from reviewers than his films had ever done before. In 1957, only two years before production began on *Psycho*, Hitchcock was the subject of an intense philosophical study of the themes of his films by the French critics Eric Rohmer and Claude Chabrol, who would themselves shortly become filmmakers.[6] In 1963, the release of *The Birds* was the culminating event in a retrospective of the director's work at the Museum of Modern Art curated by Peter Bogdonovich, another critic who would soon become a director. And in 1966, two years after *Marnie* was released, another book by a French critic-turned-director, François Truffaut's *Hitchcock,* would be published as a kind of crowning statement of a brilliant younger director on the career of a mentor and filmic giant at the very time that the study of film was becoming an academic discipline.[7]

Hitchcock's career did not remain at the peak established by these three films. After the release of *Marnie,* it went into decline: audiences, reviewers, and the studios were skeptical of the film, and thereafter he never again produced films that received the kind of critical response or success he had once enjoyed. Yet *Psycho, The Birds,* and *Marnie* collectively provided a brilliant technical coda to his career and a final period of artistic revelation that capped off what he had been showing us for more than forty years, particularly with their narratives and characters. And it was his work with the three writers and the films' screenplays that provided the framework for their success.

CHAPTER 1

The Triptych and
the Screenplays

I plan out a script very carefully, hoping to follow it exactly, all the way through, when shooting starts. In fact, this working on the script is the real making of the film, for me. When I've done it, the film is finished already in my mind.
—Alfred Hitchcock, "Direction"

I emphasize the work of Hitchcock's writers partly because they can stand as partially representative of the whole cluster of key collaborators whom criticism is accustomed to marginalise, and partly because they have such a clear and, surely, indisputable role in creating the structure within which others then work.
—Charles Barr, *English Hitchcock*

Orson Welles once said that his essential talent as a filmmaker was his instinctive ability to know exactly where the camera should be placed for maximum dramatic impact when he arrived on a set with his cast and crew. In fact, while shooting *Citizen Kane* he once sent everyone home because his instinct had failed him and he had no idea how to approach the shoot.[1] This reliance on visual intuition, especially when surrounded by other professionals waiting for direction, is precisely the opposite of Alfred Hitchcock's attitude toward the preparation necessary for effective filmmaking. "I plan out a script very carefully": this understatement serves as the basis for our study. In a very real sense, the creation of the screenplay, and ultimately the shooting script, constituted the essence of the art of filmmaking for Hitchcock. And this art necessarily entailed a close, complex collaboration between the director and his screenwriters.

Our focus is this process as it was carried out for three films and three writers and their work with the director. These films constitute what we call the "triptych" formed by *Psycho* (1960), *The Birds* (1963), and *Marnie* (1964), a grouping of films produced at a time when American culture and filmmaking were changing and the director was eager to move his films in a new direction in terms of content and technique. Technically and thematically they echo each other, and they are each centered on a female protagonist—Marion Crane, Melanie Daniels, and Marnie Edgar. Significantly, each of the three screenwriters also worked on creating the narrative of the last of these films, *Marnie,* a fact that affords a special opportunity to examine the different hands and visions that contributed to the final product. Hitchcock and his screenwriters based each screenplay on a work of popular fiction that presented excellent material for adaptation to the screen and specific individual challenges that make the process of creating the screenplay an excellent basis for the study of adaptation in Hitchcock's work.

In beginning this study of Alfred Hitchcock's collaboration with the three writers, it is important to note that entire books have been written on Hitchcock's films without once mentioning writers' names or mentioning them only in passing, as if all the stories, characters, and themes of the films were solely determined by Hitchcock himself. Of course, the average moviegoer assumes Hitchcock wrote everything; otherwise, why would we call them "Hitchcock pictures"? And the director downplayed the importance of the written word and of dialogue, in particular, when he said on many occasions that he did not want to "make pictures of people talking," a term of opprobrium he used for many contemporary Hollywood films. As he explained to Truffaut, "To me, one of the cardinal sins for a script-writer, when he runs into some difficulty, is to say, 'We can cover that by a line of dialogue.' Dialogue should simply be a sound among other sounds, just something that comes out of the mouths of people whose eyes tell the story in visual terms."[2] Perhaps even more significantly, during interviews Hitchcock was loath to give credit to the individual screenwriters who wrote the scripts of his films, describing John Michael Hayes, his writer for *Rear Window* (1954), for example, as a "radio writer," and Joseph Stefano, the writer of *Psycho* and one of the subjects of this book, as someone who essentially contributed only dialogue to that project.[3]

But students of the cinema and filmgoers cannot ignore the screenwriter's vital contribution to the success or failure of a Hitchcock film, contributions that extend beyond dialogue. While Hitchcock was not generous with his praise, some writers, such as Stefano, have reported that in unguarded moments he would praise the work and abilities of some of their predecessors. He had, by common consent, a special talent for picking his writers, and the ledger of Hitchcock's scriptwriters is as impressive as that of any director in Hollywood, or elsewhere. Beginning with Eliot Stannard and Charles Bennett in his British period, through figures such as Thornton Wilder, Dorothy Parker, Ben Hecht, Arthur Laurents, Raymond Chandler, John Michael Hayes, Maxwell Anderson, Samuel Taylor, and Ernest Lehman in America, his screenwriters were among the most accomplished authors who wrote for the movies, and many produced textbook screenplays during their collaboration with him.

Hitchcock and His Writers: A History

Hitchcock first encountered screenwriters at Islington Studios in London in the early 1920s as a young title-card designer. Many of them were American women imported from Hollywood who specialized in adding melodramatic flourishes to the source material of a film to enrich emotional plot complications and enhance the roles of star performers. While he was finding his way within his future profession, Hitchcock tried his hand at scriptwriting, using what he learned from them. When he began to function as a director in the mid-1920s, he already had a philosophy of how to adapt a source to the screen that emphasized the audience's emotional reactions: "Hitchcock always plucked out the dramatic elements that spoke to him. Then he found ways to stage these dynamic situations that would magnify their emotional impact."[4] Early on, Hitchcock realized that adapting a novel or a full-length play for the screen required a restructuring of the source narrative. He told Truffaut that a movie "is closer to a short story, which, as a rule, sustains one idea that culminates when the action has reached the highest point of the dramatic curve. As you know, a short story is rarely put down in the middle, and in this sense it resembles a film." He also makes the point that, like a play, a film must be structured by "successive climaxes."[5]

In a 1939 talk, he had already made the short-story analogy: "Now in the shape of this thing, it is inevitable that you must design your incidents and your story shape to mount up. I always think the film shape is very much like the short story. Once it starts, you haven't time to let up. You must go right through, and your film must end on its highest note. It must never go over the curve. Once you have reached your high spot, then the film is stopped."[6] Thus, as he worked closely with the writers he hired, he guided them by insisting that the script be unified by "one idea" that is developed through a series of climactic scenes, each one surpassing its predecessor in its capacity to stir the audience's emotions. From *The Lodger* (which the director considered the first "true" Hitchcock film) to *Family Plot,* the narrative structure of each of his movies can be characterized this way.

Using the short-story paradigm, Hitchcock from the beginning assumed that the successive climactic scenes should be built on images, not words. Inspired by his direct experience with the visual innovations of the revolutionary German cinema of the 1920s, he learned to create screenplays that would tell a story purely in visual terms, especially when the raw material of the story suggested rich emotional possibilities and complications. As a young director, he also found a superb confidant who understood the mechanics of screenwriting in his wife, Alma Reville, an experienced film professional who shared his cinematic vision, with its focus on emotional impact, and wrote screenplays for him in England during the late twenties and early thirties and then in America during the forties.[7] Commentators, such as the biographer Patrick McGilligan, have described her as one of "the three Hitchcocks" who created each film's screenplay, with the director and the writer as the other two.[8]

Hitchcock's collaboration with Eliot Stannard, and later with Charles Bennett, in his British period established the pattern and direction of his screenplays, as Charles Barr indicates in *English Hitchcock.* While their contributions were largely unacknowledged by the director and marginalized by scholars until recently, their input set the narrative direction of his films, not merely in the English period but later as well. The two writers provided much-needed continuity to the various episodes the director had envisioned and essential elements of character and psychology.[9] This can be seen in his 1926 adaptation of Marie Belloc Lowndes's novel *The Lodger,* in which Stannard, working closely with the young director, expanded the role of the principal female character and her relationship with the protagonist and enhanced the visual texture of the narrative with motifs such as the blond, "golden curls" of all of the killer's victims. Stannard collaborated on seven Hitchcock silent films,[10] and he helped the young director see the emotional possibilities that could be achieved by creating substantial roles for female characters and erotic relationships. It was also with Stannard that Hitchcock initiated the practice of first conceptualizing the story in detail—going over it minutely and planning its visual highlights. Frequently Hitchcock shared the concept of the film with others working on the project, telling editors, designers, cameramen, and technical people the plot as it was evolving and then using their feedback to refine it. In this way, he established the much-discussed pattern of creating a film in his mind even before the script was written, and his imaginative conception of the film was itself the product of this kind of collaboration.[11]

Early in his career, Hitchcock often shared writing credit with his scenarists; however, with the coming of sound and the need for more elaborate plotting and dialogue, the writers began to gain more autonomy. He would frequently use a number of them at various stages of a single film, each characteristically with a particular task or specialty, such as dialogue or continuity. Despite the growing importance of these specialists, Hitchcock stayed totally involved as a "writer" in the composition of the script, working with the scenarists to create suspense incrementally, thus facilitating the narrative's emotional impact upon the audience: increasing the pressure, then relieving it, only to build toward a dramatic crescendo in the third act, or conclusion, of the film.

The most influential of his writers in the British sound period was the dramatist Charles Bennett,[12] a master of creating cinematic structure and sequence and constructing characters, as evidenced in films such as *The 39 Steps,* which was based on a novel by John Buchan. As was to be his practice with screenwriters throughout the later American period, and especially during the triptych, Hitchcock formed a close, at times intense, relationship with Bennett. Working together with the director, Bennett expanded and enriched the plot and deepened the character of the novel's protagonist, Hannay. He linked his personal struggle to win exoneration and to save his country to a series of encounters with women that they invented and to a developing love relationship with a central female character, none of which is in the book. Such potential encounters and love stories, which would be intertwined with the suspense and the mystery, were to become one of Hitchcock's trademarks as a director, along with his tendency to use them to develop the protagonist's character.

So while the source material provided the essential story concept, Hitchcock and the writers took this concept in a direction that was at once cinematic and psychological, emphasizing dramatic moments and adding female characters and romantic subplots to the mix, which expanded the emotional possibilities of the narrative. Central to the latter were plot complications involving couples, their families, and oedipal relationships that dovetailed with the interplay of sex and violence. Collaborating with the writer, Hitchcock adapted the source material and wove narrative elements together into what was to become the characteristic Hitchcock narrative that established his international reputation.

This pattern within his screenplays was expanded when Hitchcock came to America, partially because of his collaboration with the producer David O. Selznick, one of whose specialties was the "woman's picture," which offered a rich new venue for Hitchcockian narrative. But by the time Hitchcock had arrived in the United States, in addition to having incorporated plot elements that involved vulnerable female and problematic male characters and their emotional relationships into his narratives, he was already adept at, and in control of, every aspect of creating a screenplay. In addition to what he had gained from his collaboration with writers such as Stannard and Bennett, he had developed a team of associates in England that he brought with him to America that included not only Alma but also Joan Harrison and others he met in the United States, such as Norman Lloyd, who understood the mechanics of building a screenplay and Hitchcock's own specific narrative tendencies and signature elements. Alma and Harrison were involved in varying degrees in four of the first American features he made, from *Rebecca* (1939) through *Shadow of a Doubt* (1943).

As Leonard Leff has shown in *Hitchcock and Selznick,* a reluctant Hitchcock, working in concert with his longtime assistant Harrison and a number of different screenwriters, shaped a screenplay for *Rebecca* that ultimately followed the producer's conception of an extremely vulnerable female protagonist that Selznick believed would appeal to a female audience. In this and in subsequent Selznick International Hitchcock films, the producer insisted upon an even more heightened attention to character and psychology than Hitchcock was accustomed to. With *Spellbound* (1945) and *Notorious* (1946), Selznick was adamant that the director and his principal screenwriter, Ben Hecht, move the narratives as much as possible in the direction of melodrama and romance and deepen the emotional lives of the characters.[13]

Hitchcock's work with established literary figures such as Thornton Wilder and John Steinbeck, and his subsequent collaborations during the 1940s with skilled Hollywood writers such as Jo Swerling and Ben Hecht, expanded his awareness of the possibilities of narrative as well as his control over the screenwriting process. Swerling, who wrote much of the screenplay for *Lifeboat* (1943), considered Hitchcock an original artistic creator who was truly the author of the narratives of his films, especially in the ways he envisioned characters, dramatic situations, and scenes.[14] With Hecht, who worked on several of Hitchcock's later films and received credit for the screenplays of *Spellbound* and *Notorious,* the director spent weeks researching and working out stories and scripts. On *Notorious,* Hitchcock even did some preliminary scriptwriting, which Hecht would then rewrite, and the two of them tailored the script to the actors who had been hired, Ingrid Bergman and Cary Grant, and keyed the dialogue to camera angles and camera positions that the director planned for crucial dramatic moments: practices that were to enrich later films, such as *Psycho.*[15]

Later in the 1950s, working with John Michael Hayes at Paramount, the director continued the same pattern of intense involvement in creating the narrative and script. On *Rear Window,* for example, Hitchcock already had decided to expand the source material before the writer began work, increasing its characterological, dramatic, and visual possibilities. Together with Hayes, he transformed the protagonist into a photographer and envisioned a rich, stylish girlfriend, who does not exist in the Woolrich story, as a love interest.[16] As Steven De Rosa shows in his treatment of the Hitchcock/Hayes collaboration on *Rear Window,* at the same time as the writer fleshed out the main character's psychology and added other characters for him to observe, he soon realized that the director's main concern was creating a love relationship for the protagonist where none exists in the source story. Hitchcock had also already selected James Stewart and Grace Kelly for the leads. The writer and the director developed the story, and while Hayes composed the dialogue, the director made clear how it should sound to suit Stewart and Kelly, and how to make their characters real and believable for the audience. In fact, when a screenplay failed to make the characters sufficiently real for him, as was the case with the initial script for *Vertigo* by Alec Coppel, Hitchcock would bring in a new writer to rewrite it. On that film, this was the task of Samuel Taylor, who added the character Midge to ground the narrative more fully in everyday reality and rewrote the dialogue to highlight the film's psychological motifs, intensify the character of Scottie, and enrich the eerie San Francisco background to the Scottie/Madeline romance. But in all of this, the writer did not work alone. Taylor maintained that he worked closely with the director on every aspect of the screenplay and always followed his lead.

Hitchcock's writers, from Charles Bennett to Ernest Lehman, have further maintained that while his films contain distinct narrative patterns, he did not always conceptualize individual films in terms of themes or even complete, fully articulated plots but as a series of scenes, situations, or "touches" that he would expect to integrate into a coherent and organic narrative.[17] Samuel Taylor characterized Hitchcock as a "short story" writer who initially thought of his films' narratives in terms of a linking of scenes and situations, and he worked with his writers to develop the screenplays within this framework.[18] In the British films, according to Taylor, one of these "situations" can be found in the poignant sequence that Charles Bennett wrote for *The 39 Steps* that features Robert Donat as the fugitive Hannay and Peggy Ashcroft as the Scottish crofter's wife.[19] The sequence displays Hannay's characteristic resourcefulness and charm, his ability to manipulate circumstances and gain the help of a sympathetic albeit vulnerable female character to facilitate his survival and to keep the narrative alive. But the episode also speaks to qualities such as openness, trust, and generosity, as opposed to suspicion, intolerance, and greed, and it presents a marital relationship that is based on a kind of literal, as well as emotional, imprisonment or shackling in contrast to the union that later develops between the handcuffed Hannay and Pamela. As Bennett articulated this "situation" under Hitchcock's guidance, Hannay's ability to gain the confidence and support of the wife foreshadows his winning the confidence, support, and love of the initially resistant Pamela. Hannay escapes and survives because of the wife's assistance, and the whole episode facilitates his becoming the hero/lover he is by the conclusion, when he successfully resolves the adventure he has been thrust into.

On a later film such as *Vertigo,* Hitchcock had, according to Taylor, chosen the film's San Francisco setting and already visualized many of the film's crucial scenes and described them to him when they began working together. Hitchcock had studied the source novel and plotted out many scenes with the previous screenwriter: the opening roof scene, the scenes at Ernie's, the Mission Delores scene, the tower scenes. He also had a strong sense of the direction of the plot, of the characters, and, most importantly, of the deeper fable that he wanted the film to communicate through the narrative and these characters—the protagonist's misguided attempt to re-create a dead love in a living woman and to transform the real into the ideal. Taylor called this level of the narrative the "story" to contrast it with the more obvious and accessible linear level, or "plot."

This deeper level was what Hitchcock and the screenwriter sought to create by enriching the narrative and deepening the characters, thereby elevating the script to a more profound human level on which the audience learns the most compelling or devastating motivations, revelations, and consequences of events. In *Vertigo,* the plot, according to Taylor, is a far-fetched, even improbable "yarn," but the story, the deeper human fable, becomes the cruelest joke that is possible to perpetrate upon a human being. It mocks his most elemental wishes and desires, turns them against him, and renders him tragic.[20]

The writer had to give precise verbal expression to this story and help create believable scenes that would not relegate the fable to a fantasy world. Hitchcock needed a writer to help ground the characters and plot in an environment that would feel genuine to the audience so that he could communicate this more profound level—a writer who would facilitate the process of audience identification and engagement, as with the crofter's scene in *The 39 Steps.* As he told Truffaut, when he created a film he intended it neither as a "slice of life" nor an "out and out fantasy" but as a "story" that is dramatic and human, with characters with whom the audience can connect. Even his technical virtuosity, he maintained, had to "enrich the action" and be "subordinated to the purpose" of the story.[21]

Throughout his British period, beginning with *The Lodger* (1926), Hitchcock's films exhibit elements of the male adventure narrative as well as more female-centered story elements, such as romance and melodrama. In some films, such as *The 39 Steps,* the former seem to dominate, while in films such as *Blackmail* (1929) the latter do. From early on, adventure, suspense, melodrama, and the potential for romance define the narratives. Once Hitchcock came to America and found himself under the aegis of Selznick, this pattern evolved. He made a number of films that, like the three of the triptych, feature female protagonists, films with characteristics of the broad genre of the woman's picture. The women in these films also go through adventures that involve solving the mystery at the heart of their narrative. But just as important is their drive to fulfill themselves emotionally, or romantically, by eliminating the impediments to this goal: *Rebecca, Suspicion, Shadow of a Doubt* (1943), and *Notorious* fit this pattern.

Different forms of narrative surround both the male and female figures in these films, specifically the more "male" form of melodrama that is characterized by risk, danger, and, most of all, suspense, and the more "female" kind of melodrama, sometimes equated with "domestic melodrama" and the woman's picture and connected more closely with the psychic struggles of the characters, their self-actualization, and their relationships. The scene with the crofter's wife in *The 39 Steps,* for example, contains both types of narrative in fairly straightforward form. Interestingly, just as characters and new episodes that enhanced story were later created for the three films, neither this scene nor the crofter's wife appears in the Buchan adventure novel that the film is adapted from; the scene was Hitchcock's and Bennett's invention. The male level of narrative is embodied in Hannay, the protagonist adventurer/actor, who is alone, hungry, and friendless when he first appears at the croft. He is being pursued by the police for a murder he did not commit, and he is struggling to find and uncover the thirty-nine steps and exonerate himself. The suspense melodrama of his situation is the product of his need to keep his identity hidden and his need to survive, especially after Margaret, the wife, discovers who he is from a newspaper story she reads in his presence.

At the same time, this scene has many of the characteristics of the kind of domestic melodrama that would be richly expanded and developed in Hitchcock's later American films. At the center of this level of the narrative is the poignant and endearing Margaret, whose courage and resourcefulness in helping the handsome, charming Hannay escape provide a fleeting moment of romance and adventure to her life, although in the process she becomes vulnerable to her life-denying husband's anger, cruelty, and punishment that we realize will be her continuing lot in life. Much of the wife's situation is revealed to the audience visually, and while she is able to help Hannay, she has little control over her own fate and will be merely a memory for him after this moment, even though her poignant, circumscribed existence continues to resonate with the audience long after she disappears from the plot. While this scene and the whole film do not add up to a "story" on the level of *Vertigo* or the films of the triptych, there is a touching human message contained within it.

The essence of the Hitchcock narrative paradigm, if we can identify it as such, is the successful integration of the tension and suspense of the mystery or adventure with the exploration of character and building of relationships that occur simultaneously. The writers understood that if they were to be successful in their part of "making" the picture with him, the director required an engaging screenplay that developed characters, created complex human connections for them, and suggested the turbulence of the protagonist's inner world. And while film cannot re-create the interior lives of characters in the way that fiction can, visual and verbal subjectivity became an increasingly prominent aspect of the narrative in Hitchcock from the 1940s onward: *Rebecca, Suspicion, Shadow of a Doubt, Spellbound,* and *Notorious* all show the evolution of this tendency toward greater subjectivity in his work, a tendency that was greatly expanded in the 1950s films—*Strangers on a Train, Rear Window, Vertigo, North by Northwest*—and that is at the heart of the triptych of *Psycho, The Birds,* and *Marnie.*

Stefano, Hunter, and Allen

Each of the screenwriters for the triptych we are examining was working for the first time with Hitchcock and was relatively new to screenwriting and to the visual images he created—a fact that makes their collaboration with him appropriate for this kind of study. It is unclear whether Hitchcock felt that this would give him more control over the narrative, but he clearly looked on each collaboration as something of a teaching experience. Despite the evident limit of their experience and screenplay credits, Hitchcock was confident that he had selected three writers who were suited to the demands of the specific narratives for each film or what he wanted the screenplay to bring to light. Either he found something compelling in the writer's personality and previous work that dovetailed with what he hoped to achieve in the project, or something about the young author's initial creative suggestions struck him as inventive and in accord with his own goals. In addition, at this stage of his career, the director seemed to want to work with writers who were new to Hollywood and "the industry," who didn't bring with them ideas and assumptions nurtured by the studio system.

As was his pattern with previous authors, his working rapport with these writers helped to make them secure and comfortable as collaborators. He quickly formed a personal relationship with each. With Stefano it centered on their mutual interests, such as English music-hall performers of the past and the psychoanalysis the writer was undergoing at the time he was working on the *Psycho* screenplay, an experience that Stefano freely shared with the director.[22] *Psycho* is steeped in the insights of psychoanalysis, though they mostly came from Stefano, not Hitchcock. The writer maintained, "We discussed my analysis. He wanted to know what was going on there, but he had no background in Freud. He said he had never spoken to anyone who admitted to being in psychoanalysis. I liked the way he accented 'admitted.' He thought it was kind of wild of me to admit this. He was really interested. Sometimes I would tell him things I didn't even tell my analyst! If they applied to the screenplay in some way, I would tell him about it." In a similar way, Hitchcock's relationship with Hunter quickly became an active social relationship that involved their wives and reciprocal dinners, all part of Hitchcock's attempt to play host and paterfamilias to the writer's young family that had moved out to Los Angeles to be with him. At times, Hitchcock could be demanding, overbearing, and even inappropriate, according to Hunter, but the writer never lost his fondness for him.[23] The relationship with Allen, who was completely new to Hollywood, centered on Hitch and Alma literally taking her into their home as a member of the family. Allen was especially impressed by their warmth and generosity, and by Alma's savvy and judgment where people were concerned.[24]

All three reported that in working sessions it sometimes seemed as if Hitchcock would tell stories and off-color jokes and recount Hollywood gossip more than he would discuss the film they were working on, a phenomenon that, while it could be exasperating, put them at ease, especially when they seemed stuck on some issue in the narrative. Since each was new to screenwriting, Hitchcock needed them to understand the filmmaking process as thoroughly as possible and especially his particular vision for the story and how it should be told. He accomplished this in part by giving them each what they felt was the best film education they ever received, much of it coming from them watching his previous films and then discussing them in detail. This was especially true with Stefano and Allen, less so with Hunter, who soon left Los Angeles and their daily meetings to finish the screenplay of *The Birds* in the East. Interestingly, during our interviews, the three writers, each of whom wrote a film with a heroine as its protagonist, all chose as a personal favorite among the Hitchcock films one that has a female protagonist: for Stefano it was a toss-up between *Rebecca* and *Vertigo*; for Hunter and Allen it was *Notorious*.

What drew Hitchcock to these three writers, collectively and individually? All three were relatively young (Stefano was thirty seven, Hunter thirty five, Allen forty) and new to filmmaking. Each was outgoing, social, direct, and not timid about offering ideas and approaches, qualities Hitchcock liked; and while they were delighted to be working with Hitchcock, none was in awe of him. They also seemed to the director to be attuned to American culture, which he needed them to bring to the screenplays, especially since there was a sense in Hollywood in the early 1960s that audiences were changing and that younger viewers, in particular, wanted to see films that reflected their lives and values. Accordingly, Hitchcock brought the three writers into the actual production process of the film: on *Marnie,* in particular, he had the writer meet with him and the production people to work out the design and shape of the film while the screenplay was being written. In addition, he sent them out to learn essential background information and to scout out locations and get atmosphere for what they were writing, and he asked them on occasion to communicate aspects of the characters they were creating to the actors.

They all were eager to learn from and collaborate with an artist they had long respected and admired, and each seemed to have a quality or ability that connected them to the specific project. Stefano was distinctly psychologically minded, and he had a special proclivity for the psychology of parent-child interaction, which had played a significant role in *The Black Orchid.* Although he initially did not like the darkness and squalid ambience of the novel and seemed disappointed that *Psycho* was to be "his Hitchcock picture," the character of Norman Bates and the sexual undercurrent of the material, with its link to "Mother" and sadism, intrigued him and were actually tailor-made for him. In fact, toward the end of his life, Stefano was working on a play called *Psycho/Analysis* that dramatizes the interaction of his collaboration with Hitchcock and his own therapy to come to terms with his own sadistic drives.

Hunter prided himself on his ability to adapt and "open up" or expand the subjective and psychological possibilities of the source material, which he had done when composing the script for Hitchcock's television show, and he had also written science fiction. He would draw upon these experiences to update and translate the short story "The Birds" to an American setting and the screen. And while Allen's work with Hitchcock was her entrance into scriptwriting, she was soon to become one of a handful of pioneering women screenwriters who achieved notable success in Hollywood in the 1960s, 1970s, and 1980s. Hitchcock hired her for *Marnie* because of the frankness, directness, and subtlety of her stage adaptation of the novel *The Prime of Miss Jean Brodie,* especially her handling of complex sexual motifs that were so crucial to his conception of *Marnie,* and because he felt she would bring a "woman's point of view" to the project.

The three writers wrote these films with Hitchcock in a period of less than four years, in many ways a compressed period of time, especially when one considers the three-year hiatus between the releases of *Psycho* and *The Birds*. After completing *North by Northwest,* Hitchcock had begun work on a film with Samuel Taylor as the scenarist with the title "No Bail for the Judge," which was never produced. As an alternative, the director had decided to film *Psycho* in April 1959, shortly after reading the Robert Bloch novel by the same title, envisioning it as a feature film that would essentially follow the narrative format of his television show, *Alfred Hitchcock Presents,* and share its production techniques. After dismissing the initial writer on the project, who had composed what he felt was an unsatisfactory script, he reluctantly agreed to meet with Joseph Stefano and have him try his hand at the screenplay, although he did not think much of *The Black Orchid* and considered it too much of a social-problem film. Stefano met Hitchcock at his studio trailer for the first time on September 1, 1959, when he listened favorably to the writer's idea that the first part of the film should focus on Marion. The writer submitted his first draft of *Psycho* in October 1959, which received the director's approval, and several revised drafts followed in the next two months. Principal photography began on November 30, the shooting was completed by February 1, and the film was released on June 16, 1960. The astounding critical controversy and popular success that followed seem to have convinced Hitchcock that the follow-up would have to extend some aspect of *Psycho*'s narrative and technical innovations.

After discussing several ideas with his collaborators and even with the media in the months following *Psycho*'s tumultuous release, Hitchcock decided to explore further the dark sexuality he had introduced in it by adapting Winston Graham's 1961 novel *Marnie,* a study of the erotic neuroses of a compulsive thief. He was already in contact with Grace Kelly, who had become a princess in Monaco, about coming out of retirement to play the part, something that strongly appealed to the director and to Universal, the studio he had just moved to. Joseph Stefano, whose own psychoanalysis had been so indispensable in writing *Psycho,* had the personal experience and technical knowledge needed for such a study. He was asked by the director to repeat his success by writing an initial treatment of *Marnie* that presumably he would expand into a screenplay after story conferences with Hitchcock. Stefano was sent the novel early in 1961, and he submitted his lengthy treatment in June. By then, however,

Princess Grace had decided to postpone her celebrated return to Hollywood, and the project was dropped for the time being. But to understand the interrelationships among the three films of the triptych, it is important to note that *Marnie* was directly linked to *Psycho* in the director's mind. The aborted project was a significant cause of the unusually long three-year delay between the release of back-to-back Hitchcock features.

By the summer of 1961, Hitchcock had decided to move on and adapt Daphne du Maurier's short story "The Birds," a 1952 work that he had included in his 1959 anthology, *My Favorites in Suspense*. After Stefano declined the project because of a phobia about birds, and after interviewing several other writers who did not work out, Hitchcock hired the well-known and versatile novelist Evan Hunter in August 1961 to write the script. He asked Hunter to completely revamp the story, to adapt it to an American setting that he had already picked out in Bodega Bay, California, and to make it cinematic; by November he had a first-draft screenplay in hand. Hunter's draft went through a number of redrafts and second-guesses about characterization by Hitchcock before production began in February 1962, and the daunting special effects meant that production and postproduction lasted much longer than was typical for Hitchcock; consequently, *The Birds* was not completed until the end of the summer. It was finally released in March 1963.

Even during the shooting of *The Birds* in the spring of 1962, Hitchcock began work again on *Marnie,* at a time when there was still some hope of luring Grace Kelly back for the principal role. He started discussing the project not with Joseph Stefano, who had moved on to a television show he was co-creating, *The Outer Limits,* but with the rehired Evan Hunter, and official story conferences for *Marnie* began in the fall and extended into February 1963. Hunter worked closely with the director on the project, even conducting background interviews with psychiatrists to create the main character; however, he experienced with Hitchcock the disappointment of Grace Kelly's final withdrawal from the film that year. After struggling with a scene in the novel that he was uncomfortable with, Hunter submitted two versions of a first draft in April, one including the so-called rape scene, and one without it, the version Hunter himself strongly preferred. As a result of their difference over this scene, Hitchcock dismissed Hunter from the project, and they never worked together again.

Jay Presson Allen was hired to take over the writing in May 1963 and spent the next four months in story conferences with Hitchcock and on the new script, which used some of Hunter's ideas (though she did not know who had written what the director showed her) while dramatically altering several of the main characters in the Graham book and Hunter's screenplay. The final shooting script is dated October 1963. Some shooting had begun in September, though principal photography began in November. The film wrapped in March and was released in June 1964. Thus the work on Hitchcock's last great period began in 1959 and was finally completed five years later in 1964.

When he began working with them, the director discussed narrative choices with the writers and took pains to share his vision of the overall direction of the plot and how specific scenes in the diegesis would look in the finished film. Yet, in these three works, as in each of Hitchcock's films, the writers did the actual writing. As Hitchcock told Joseph Stefano, "You write the script. We'll talk it all out. I want to know where it's all going, but you decide what they'll say." "And unlike a lot of directors who tell you that and then hit you over the head," Stefano added, "he really did mean it. . . . I would try out scenes [that I thought up] on him, and he would react. But he was visualizing the movie, making it in his head . . . and if he could see how you could cut from this sequence to that sequence, or scene, he would be happy. [But] he did not want to be bothered by any kinds of character motivation." By this point in the process of creating the screenplay, Hitchcock had assumed the role of director, not co-writer, and creating dialogue was for him the writer's domain.[25]

Postwar America: Hitchcock and the 1950s

Hitchcock always strongly desired to connect the plots of his films to the contemporary culture. With his critical reputation approaching its peak during the years the three writers worked with him, he had already directed many of his most critically acknowledged films during the previous decade, the 1950s: an era defined internationally and domestically by the cold war, McCarthyism, and a pervasive mood of repression that American cultural historians have connected to an obsession with conformity, containment, and consensus.[26] Robert J. Corber argues that during this period, the director's films "participated in the dominant system of representation" but simultaneously revealed the inadequacy of "the [contemporary] liberal interpretation of reality and thus threatened to destabilize or rupture it."[27] In other words, while films such as *The Man Who Knew Too Much* (1956) and *North by Northwest* seem superficially to present and even promote the middle-class world, lifestyle, and values of the McKennas and Roger Thornhill, the narrative context these characters are placed within reveals their contradictions and inadequacy.

In a similar way, *Psycho, The Birds,* and *Marnie,* all produced between 1959 and 1964, are less linked to and reflective of the so-called radical sixties than they are of the more controlled fifties and possess more cultural texture of this earlier era, in which the three screenwriters came of age as writers. They contain traces of the historical events and of the change that marked this "liberalizing" five-year period that is associated with the promise of the short-lived Kennedy administration and some the tensions of the period, such as the fear of nuclear war. But these three works seem more rooted in the earlier decade: *Psycho* (1960) is actually the last work the director produced in the 1950s, a creative period that witnessed a number of his most culturally complex films: *Strangers on a Train, Rear Window, The Man Who Knew Too Much, Vertigo,* and *North by Northwest.*

Each of these earlier 1950s films resonated with American cold-war and 1950s culture, and much of this resonance was the contribution of the screenwriter who collaborated with Hitchcock. It is this culture more than cold-war politics that is at the heart of each as a product of its time. Many contemporary social and cultural tensions reverberate through them, tensions that were reflective of the insecurity, anxiety, and even paranoia generated in the larger domestic and global political arena. It is too facile to see Hitchcock as simply reflecting and validating contemporary social values or, conversely, as critiquing and exposing them within his narratives. The reality is that these values were embedded in his films, equally the product of what his writers and the director brought to the screenplays.

Beginning with *Psycho,* Hitchcock's three films after the end of the 1950s were produced at a time when the international situation was perhaps more volatile than it had been since the end of the Second World War, and American domestic life was beginning to undergo its greatest cultural upheaval since the 1930s. The intensity of these films is in part the result of the impact of historical events of the period of their creation at the height of the cold war. These years witnessed the election of John F. Kennedy and the Bay of Pigs invasion; the Berlin Wall and blockade; the acceleration of the civil rights movement with its freedom rides, violence against civil-rights activists (a number of whom were murdered), and voting rights for African Americans; the rise of Fidel Castro and the Cuban Missile Crisis; the assassination of the Vietnamese president Ngo

Din Diem and the expansion of the Vietnam War; and, perhaps most troublingly, the Kennedy assassination. All of these events were played out against a pervasive fear of a nuclear conflagration that would have ended American culture and life in general.

Yet the three films did not intersect explicitly with contemporary history or these developments, just as the director's films of the previous decade had remained aloof from historical specificity. Instead, Hitchcock and his three screenwriters engaged cold-war culture in relation to psychological issues, and to an extent sexual politics. It was the social and cultural stresses of this era that most interested Hitchcock: the impact that this turbulent history was having on individual lives and relationships. As Charles Barr states, the "importance of Hitchcock derives, in large part, from his sensitivity to the social and cultural currents of the time and place in which he was operating, and from his ability to dramatize these at a profound level, particularly in terms of sexual politics."[28]

Such stresses can best be understood with an awareness that psychological explanations of behavior, psychological remedies, and a new frankness about sexuality were hallmarks of a developing therapeutic culture that was central to the ethos of the late 1950s and the early 1960s, which the screenwriters indirectly drew upon. As part of this therapeutic culture, American society became engaged in a new discourse about psychology and mental health and a culture of expertise in which psychologists, psychiatrists, and psychoanalysts played leading roles. A new kind of psychotherapy was developing that was psychoanalytically informed and dynamically minded, seeking to improve a patient's understanding and functioning and, on the broadest level, the quality of American life. It was closer to classical psychoanalysis than to behaviorism in its emphasis on the primacy of relationships with parents as influences on adult development, but it was not without behavioristic elements. This therapeutic culture agreed with Freud that love and work are the cornerstones of individual humanity, and that achieving fulfillment in both makes one a complete human being, as Abraham Maslow's concept of self-actualization would articulate by the mid-1960s. It was perhaps more Jungian than Freudian in its positive view of the human condition and in its belief in the possibility of personal change, growth, and happiness, and its strongest proponents were figures such as Erik Erikson, Erich Fromm, Rollo May, Carl Rogers, Fritz Perls, and Maslow. They advocated the idea that finding positive role models, pursuing personal creativity, accepting responsibility for one's actions, and forming strong, healthy sexual relationships are just as important to personal psychic healing as the self-knowledge that comes from the classical analytic process.

The screenplay of *Psycho,* for example, includes dialogue and stage directions that focus upon the psychological struggles and analysis of the characters in contemporary therapeutic terms; similarly, the family dynamic and parent-child relations are at the center of *The Birds,* and there are references to "Oedipus" as a term of explanation in the script; and *Marnie* is a film steeped in contemporary psychological values and ideas. In fact, one of the first two major studies of Hitchcock's work, that of Robin Wood (1965), published the year after *Marnie* was released, argued that the director's films were first and foremost a profound psychological exploration of the human condition and that his 1950s films and those of the triptych are explicitly "therapeutic."[29] Each of the three films that are the focus of this book was to have such a therapeutic dimension in its narrative.

It is important to note that the 1950s were the decade of the impact of the *Kinsey Reports* on sexual behavior (1948, 1953), which had created controversy, particularly the open treatment of female sexuality in the 1953 volume, at a time when cultural historians widely regarded America as a repressed society. In *Psycho,* for example, the desperation epitomized by Marion and Sam at the film's opening and the underlying theme of repression in their relationship resonates in terms of the American 1950s and cold-war culture, alongside the openness about Marion's sexuality and the film's sexual directness. During the 1950s, sexual repression and desperation had received touching treatment in the films of Douglas Sirk, in the plays of Tennessee Williams and William Inge, and in popular novels such as Grace Metalious's *Peyton Place;*[30] Joseph Stefano's screenplay tapped into the same cultural vein. The poignant postcoital opening of *Psycho* has a covert, dark, forbidden quality that underscores the way much of 1950s American sexuality was represented. As Stefano was aware, this scene contains an aura of something dark and forbidden. The audience is let in on a part of Marion that she has hidden from her family, her employer, her coworkers, and to some degree herself. Sex is mixed with pathos in Marion; in her female co-worker, played by Pat Hitchcock, it is suppressed with tranquilizers (a foreshadowing of the pill culture that was to develop in America). Marion almost appears ready to give sex up, since she cannot experience it respectably within marriage, just as the strapping, attractive Sam regards their afternoon pleasure with wistful resignation.

Closely related to this theme of repressed and frustrated sexuality is the film's presentation of social class and economic issues. The film presents three fictional characters living in what were then primary migratory locales for the American dream—California and Arizona—places to which 1950s Americans were relocating in search of the good life. But Marion's womanhood is thwarted there, and Sam's masculinity is challenged and undercut. Both attribute the inertia in their relationship to a lack of money, a deficiency that motivates Marion's desperate act and prevents Sam from marrying her. Joseph Stefano had included further references to their social and economic inadequacies, which the director cut during filming.

On an even more profound scale, repression and social class define the character of Norman Bates, who represented Hitchcock's most innovative and daring statement about the dark side of American culture to date. However, Norman lives more on the sexual and economic margins of the culture than Marion and Sam do. To use the sheriff's words, he "lives like a hermit," running a failing motel that attracts a trickle of customers each month because the highway has been "moved." The sparseness of his existence—emblematized by his antiquated surroundings and possessions and his thrifty and austere habits—has fed his psychosis, which in turn has alienated him from the postwar consumer culture that, as a motel owner, he is supposed to be an integral part of and, more importantly, from his fellow human beings. On a material level, his life is starker than Marion's and Sam's working-class existence, and on the level of sexual repression his psychosis makes their problems seem commonplace.

Beyond the obvious emotional unhappiness of all three, neither this sympathetic but put-upon couple nor this withdrawn, sensitive young man are enjoying the new prosperity that historians have connected with this period, or that film audiences habitually associated with the comfortable living standards of Hitchcock's usual characters. Yet, as was the Hollywood practice, Hitchcock, Stefano, and the actors represent all three as physically attractive people, thereby accentuating visually the seeming injustice of this set of circumstances. Marion, in addition to her physical appeal, seems more dignified and well-spoken in the film's dialogue than her occupation or social standing would account for, and Norman seems to possess a more considered understanding of himself and of the human condition in general than his personal and economic situation would suggest. These ironic discrepancies, like the desperate circumstances of all three, link them still further, and in Norman's case they add a dimension to his madness that is at once terrifying and compelling.

Hitchcock's next film, which we believe should have followed *Marnie,* was *The Birds,* which is still enormously popular, second only to *Psycho.* With its narrative centered upon a force that threatens total devastation, it has perhaps the most obvious cold-war resonance of any of the three films, and many viewers seeing it for the first time read it as an allegory about nuclear war. In the section on *The Birds* in his book of interviews with Hitchcock, Truffaut brought up the film's obvious contemporary historical association: "Since 1945, it's the atom bomb that has represented the ultimate threat to mankind, so it's rather disconcerting to suggest that the end of the world might be brought about by thousands of birds."[31] However, during production the director deliberately sought to minimize and suppress the historical and cultural associations that Evan Hunter had woven into the screenplay. Hitchcock and Hunter had different conceptions of what the bird attacks should signify. Despite possibilities for political allegory and their presence in the source story, Hitchcock chose to foreground the personal and psychological rather than the political in the film, emphasizing the primacy of emotional and psychic forces over all others. As a result, connections to America's cold-war and nuclear fears of 1963 went through a process of displacement as the script evolved. Hunter's screenplay went through numerous revisions in the three years *The Birds* took to produce. He had treated cold-war or political issues in his fiction before this experience, and they were initially part of his agenda for the film. While earlier versions of Hunter's screenplay contained references to contemporary American or world issues, Hitchcock systematically erased such historical traces from the film and focused instead on technical challenges and the enhancement of the characters as the project progressed.

While *Psycho* was written and produced at the end of the 1950s, the conclusion of the Eisenhower years, *The Birds* was a product of the short-lived Kennedy era. As Joseph Stefano remarked about the time period that produced *Psycho,* "We were at the end of the repressive fifties and were glad they were over."[32] Evan Hunter, who joined the project of *The Birds* in 1961, the year following Kennedy's election, was only thirty-four at the time and identified with the young president, his "new" energetic style, and the potential thaw in the cold war that he promised.[33] As an individual and as a writer, Evan Hunter shared some of the idealism and contradictions that appeared in Kennedy's administration and initiatives. A Second World War veteran who defined himself as being "of the left" and his politics as "extremely liberal,"[34] Hunter had, as indicated earlier, attracted attention and achieved success with *The Blackboard Jungle* (1954) and, beginning in 1956, under the pseudonym Ed McBain, with the 87th Precinct novels. Neither of these achievements would have superficially identified him as an antiwar "liberal." *The Blackboard Jungle* was based on Hunter's brief stint as an inner-city high-school teacher and chronicled the frustrations of an idealistic young teacher who learns painful life lessons as he attempts to educate resistant, underprivileged youth in an urban vocational school. Similarly, the 87th Precinct series began with *Cop Hater,* a novel in which city police, who a decade later would become one of the most visibly disparaged symbols of authority, are humanized and presented as misunderstood and, at times, victimized—a tendency that increased as the series advanced. Not surprisingly, the characters Hunter created in *The Birds* do not depart from popular gender or class stereotypes of the late 1950s, and unlike their counterparts in *Psycho,* they are all solidly upper-middle class and without economic worries. With the possible exception of the committed, self-sacrificing Annie Hayward, the Bodega Bay schoolteacher who is carrying a torch for Mitch Brenner, all of the major characters conform to classical Hollywood constructions in this regard. But Hunter did put explicit contemporary references to the precarious world situation into his earlier drafts that do not appear in the finished film.

Unlike *The Birds,* which evoked cold-war fears and politics in its allegorical narrative, *Marnie* was focused directly on individual psychology and sexuality, which were dominant topics of this period, albeit, like *Psycho,* from a different area of cold-war culture: what we have identified as "therapeutic culture." There are some connections between Marion and Marnie in this respect, and Marnie's pathology even bears comparison with Norman's. Allen benefitted from the work Hitchcock had done with Hunter, who was himself influenced by a treatment for *Marnie* that Stefano had written; and all three brought their own take on contemporary psychotherapy, some of which relied on research that they did at the time, to the conception of the repressed, frigid, criminal Marnie. The film's screenplay was composed by the third writer, Jay Presson Allen, whom the director hired, in part, to add a "woman's touch" to what was to be a melodrama about the dysfunctional compulsive thief and the man who attempts to "cure" her. The understanding and presentation of sexuality and frigidity in *Marnie* and of criminal sexual pathology reflected widely held views of the period, although Kinsey's research had actually shown that more American women were sexually active and were enjoying sex than were frigid like Marnie, and Kinsey was soon superseded by Masters and Johnson, whose findings challenged not only the presentation of frigidity in the film but the basic concept in general, placing more blame on male, rather than female, inadequacy as the cause of sexual dysfunction. So it is not surprising that contemporary reviewers did not find its presentation of the healing of a sexually damaged female thief innovative.

Significantly, while Marnie is the troubled character whose illness needs to be understood and treated, the Mark of Allen's screenplay and the film approaches the masculine ideal of the contemporary period, in relation both to Hitchcock's oeuvre and to the social theory of the time. As Allen characterized him, he displays little of the compromised and insecure manhood of Hitchcock's earlier 1950s male protagonists, who seem to suffer from the postwar crisis of masculinity that cultural critics saw infecting American society. Instead, Mark embodies the masculine virtues valorized by American popular culture, values that could be linked historically to the ruling elite to which he belongs and that were embodied in the young President Kennedy. Chief among these are competitiveness, assertive leadership, social confidence, and an aura of chivalry. Allen depicts Mark as a strong, genteel patriarch who epitomizes sagacity and determination at the same time as he rebels against the expectations and restrictions of his social class.[35] He is wealthy, handsome, and impulsive and possesses what he himself calls "healthy animal lust." He is not afraid to take risks as a businessman or as a zoologist, and he is as completely self-assured in his personal life as he is as Marnie's husband/therapist. While he is clearly smitten with Marnie, he never allows her to manipulate him and is always in charge of their relationship, thus preserving and remaining within the prescribed gender boundaries that were still the norm of the dominant culture. Because of Mark's decisiveness and confidence, Marnie's future is much less uncertain at the film's end than it is in the book, in which she is resigned to the possibility that she may have to go to jail. Thus, politically and culturally, this Mark possesses the understanding, protective, and curative qualities to appeal to contemporary liberals and the almost instinctive take-charge authority to impress conservatives.[36] But Allen also made him a problematic figure, and there is a suggestion that he may be a victim of the very values he seems to epitomize: his masculine need to take charge and control simultaneously controls and limits him.[37]

Whether Allen, who got on extremely well with the director and shared his quirky sense of humor, actually provided the female perspective that Hitchcock hoped for in *Marnie* is debatable. But she was adept at handling sexual themes and had no difficulty writing the "rape" scene that Hitchcock wanted, a scene that she did not consider an actual rape.[38] Ultimately it was her screenplay that had to represent Mark's assertive masculinity and Marnie's frigidity and thievery in ways that reflected contemporary American attitudes on psychology, sexuality, and criminology, which to a large extent it did. She also elevated the novel's social setting to conform to more traditional Hollywood expectations. But despite its sexual theme, the film essentially reflected and embodied contemporary cultural values and gender boundaries and did not challenge them or attempt to break new ground.

Allen's work on *Marnie* and the contemporary cultural resonance of the characters originated with the film's source; the same was true for the other two writers on their films. Each of the three screenwriters started with a source that the director had selected, and in each case this source had narrative and character possibilities typical of his long array of films and some that reflected new interests or tendencies. The three selected sources allowed the director and the writers to expand the possibilities of character along the cultural lines indicated above and to expand narrative in new and more provocative ways. Taken together, each source was a starting point for extending the boundaries and intensity of what the director had done previously, and its specific adaptation was intended to create a film that would move his work in a new direction.

CHAPTER 2

The Sources

An examination of how Hitchcock and his writers transformed the sources he chose reveals two tendencies that are important in
understanding how the director and the three writers went about adapting their sources into films.[1] The first tendency has to do with Hitchcock's
attitude toward adaptation and the viability and literary stature of the
works he chose; the second with the genres he characteristically drew
from. For throughout his career, Hitchcock focused on source material—
plays, novels, and short stories—that used to be called "suspense fiction"
but today is usually classified by bookstores and reviewers as "crime novels," sources tailor-made for his thrillers.[2]

As his American period advanced and he was able to get out from under
the control of David O. Selznick, Hitchcock increasingly adapted sources
the way he had his later British successes, such as John Buchan's *The 39
Steps*: using the original suspense or crime narrative as a point of departure, or framework, and adding to it, subtracting from it, and changing
the story and principal characters, not to mention its focus or tone. The
resulting film would subsume the literary original as an artistic and cultural
document to the point that Hitchcock became virtual owner of the work
and title; so, for example, *Strangers on a Train* and, later, *Psycho* became
filmic works by Alfred Hitchcock, or Hitchcock films, based on source novels of the same title by Patricia Highsmith and Robert Bloch, respectively.

From the 1950s to the period of the triptych—with the greater artistic
freedom Hitchcock received from Hollywood studios after he had severed ties with Selznick—he would reshape works of crime fiction with
greater and greater license, while still drawing upon some of the narrative
elements and generic conventions of the women's picture that he had
learned from Selznick. *Rear Window* and *Vertigo,* with their emphasis
on the protagonist's psychic life, the roles of women, and on romantic
relationships, are the best examples of this process during this period.
Equally important was making the protagonists as sympathetic as possible

to facilitate audience identification with them. In the case of the triptych, *Psycho* and *Marnie* are based on recent popular fiction, by Robert Bloch and Winston Graham, respectively, that fit the crime-novel categorization quite comfortably, though the former leans toward the "horror" end of the this wide spectrum, while the latter would be more precisely defined as a "psychological thriller."[3] The source for *The Birds,* the du Maurier short story, has elements of fable, horror, and science fiction and departs from the crime genre, and it received the most thoroughgoing transformation of the three works as far as characters and relationships are concerned, revealing the extent to which this process could go, while still retaining much of the visual fabric of the original. The novel *Psycho,* by contrast, received the least alteration.

When the director turned to his new television project, *Alfred Hitchcock Presents,* in the 1950s, he began to explore more bizarre entries in the crime-story genre, short fiction that emphasized shock, horror, and even the supernatural, qualities Hitchcock would bring to bear on the three films. Meanwhile, the source material for his 1950s feature films stayed largely within his established parameters: *Dial M for Murder, Rear Window, The Man Who Knew Too Much,* and *To Catch a Thief* all rely on the kind of sources Hitchcock was quite familiar with, while the one original script, *North by Northwest,* was largely an update of *The 39 Steps.*[4] But by the decade's end, the success of the TV show prompted Hitchcock to expand his vision of what extremes of human behavior his films could explore. All three of the writers he chose for the triptych were of a generation that recognized television not only as a fact of life but as an opportunity for their careers, and having come of age during the Second World War, they were attuned to extreme and shocking subject matter.

While he was completing *North by Northwest* and before he turned to *Psycho,* Hitchcock began an adaptation of a 1952 English thriller by Henry Cecil, *No Bail for the Judge,* a source that would allow him to explore such a behavioral extreme. He envisioned Audrey Hepburn in the lead role as the daughter of a renowned London barrister who sets out to prove the innocence of a "wrong man," her father, who in the novel has been accused of killing a prostitute. The plot has overtones of previous English successes in the Hitchcock canon, particularly *Blackmail* (1929), only this time in more extreme form, since Hitchcock and the screenwriter Samuel Taylor added a scene in which the protagonist is forced to fend off a sexual attack. However, the studio objected to it, and reportedly so did Hepburn, who dropped out of the project anyway because she became pregnant. But the choice of this potentially more intense source and the direction of its planned adaptation point toward the kind of material he chose for the triptych and the way he was to transform it.

Like *North by Northwest* (which the director admitted was an "American *39 Steps*") and *The Man Who Knew Too Much, No Bail for the Judge* would have been a reworking of familiar material—but this time with the addition of more explicit sex and violence. When the project was aborted, the director moved toward new sources for his next three films that, while increasing the allotment of sex and and/or violence, also dealt with macabre or bizarre situations typical of his television show but new to his feature films. They featured "normal," or conventional, 1950s characters with fairly ordinary, even complacent attitudes toward their lives, lives that were dramatically and cruelly destabilized—like those of the protagonists of *The Wrong Man* (1957) and *North by Northwest,* but in even more bizarre fashion. Thus, while he and the writers expanded many of the characterological possibilities these works offered, they intensified their more extreme material. Interestingly, *Psycho,* the first of these works, was produced as if it were being made for television, down to being shot in black and white. The director was attracted by the chance to pursue and extend the darker directions the novel offered, as in the shower scene, as well as the characters he had created.

Psycho

"Then the horror wasn't in the house,"
Lila murmured. "It was in his head."
—Robert Bloch, *Psycho*

Robert Bloch's *Psycho* (1959) offered Hitchcock a source to adapt with both intense and rising suspense and a central character whose crimes could expand the boundaries of screen horror. At the same time, its austere and contained settings could accommodate the technical and production scale of the television format he was intent on employing. A protégé of the American horror writer H. P. Lovecraft, Bloch (1917–94) was a successful pulp writer who, beginning in the 1930s, had specialized in crime, horror, science fiction, and historical or semihistorical tales of crime and terror. His novel works like one of the episodes on *Alfred Hitchcock Presents*: steadily increasing strangeness in a plot that leads to a shocking revelation about the possibilities of human behavior. It had been reviewed favorably in the *New York Times,* where it came to the attention of Hitchcock's staff.

Yet as a novel, *Psycho* suffers from conflicting goals: Bloch wants to give his case study a literary patina, so he uses the symbol of "darkness" and the turgid depths of the swamp to suggest the intensity of Norman Bates's derangement, but his prose doesn't support these tentative psychological probings: his short, clipped sentences when he describes Norman's thoughts; his use of italics to signal heightened moments of shock; and his breathless, cliffhanger chapter endings all heighten the horrific melodrama but downplay the characters' complexity and the possibilities of audience identification. Bloch strives to mislead his audience into assuming that Mother is really present on the scene, so as to provide surprise as well as horror as the novel draws to a close. Thus, when Hitchcock began the process of adaptation even before Joseph Stefano entered the project in September 1959, he was already looking for ways to deal with Mother and, more importantly, to make Norman more complex and compelling for the audience and to expand the possibilities of empathy and identification throughout. Joseph Stefano's guiding principle for the adaptation—to begin the narrative with Mary/Marion, to make her the main character and then move on to Norman—made this possible.

Oddly enough, it was Bloch who had first made Norman a more psychologically complex character than the actual figure he is based upon. As is well known, Norman's genesis can be traced back to Ed Gein, a serial murderer in rural Wisconsin who committed his crimes during the mid-1950s.[5] After Gein was arrested in 1957, his horrific crimes were made public in a series of local newspaper stories and television reports and seemed to be the kind of material that Hitchcock was looking for at this time. Bloch based his novel loosely around these accounts and his own onsite research. But the horror of Gein's crimes went far beyond anything Norman commits in the book, or anything that Stefano later put into the screenplay. Ironically, the Norman who slashes Marion to death in the shower and Arbogast on the staircase is a much more recognizably human figure than Gein was, and Norman's crimes are far less shocking. Although only two homicides could be directly traced to Gein, the "real" Norman had possibly killed and dismembered more than ten women, skinned many of their bodies, and severed and preserved their body parts, some of which, like their breasts, he wore around the remote farmhouse where he lived by himself. Other body parts that he saved, such as pelvic bones, he turned into lamps and other bizarre artifacts, and he used the skin he collected for drums, lampshades, and upholstery.[6] He also confessed to digging up the bodies of dead women at a local cemetery.

Most perplexing to Gein's local Wisconsin community of Plainfield was the knowledge that for many years he was considered a harmless local eccentric, trusted with odd jobs and even with babysitting. Local news stories, however, were careful not to present the most bizarre and gruesome details of his crimes. Although they acknowledged an unspecified number of actual murders and some details of dismemberment and hinted at the possibilities of cannibalism, there was scant mention of the physical evidence that the police had discovered and what it suggested about Gein, including hints of an incestuous relationship with his mother and the possible murder of a brother.[7]

Bloch initially thought that the mother-fixated Gein and his murders would make for a book that would shock and mesmerize readers, at the same time as it would extend the boundaries of what might be presented in crime fiction. Initially, Bloch was surprised that the impulse of the local journalists and television reporters was to cover up or even deny the severity of the crimes, and he wanted to make their inability to deal with them the centerpiece of the story. He had planned to explore the irony of how such a frightening mass murderer had blended so seamlessly into the small town where he lived, where his crimes had remained undetected for years, despite the fact that supposedly everyone knew everyone else's business.

Yet even after researching the case in some depth and determining to make the denial of its horror part of his focus, Bloch ultimately decided to pare down the horror of Gein's crimes in ways that were compatible with 1950s therapeutic culture and popular Freudianism, and with contemporary fears about the excesses and boundaries of mothering. Bloch's Norman is, in every way, more recognizably human than Ed Gein, and, by extension, so are his crimes.

Bloch's novel immediately introduces the reader to this more humanized Norman Bates and his bizarre, but orderly, world by bringing us inside Norman's mind and point of view. Forty, overweight, balding, pink-faced, semi-alcoholic, and mother-dominated, he is obsessed with the violent and sadistic; as the book begins, he is reading a study of the Incas that describes how they flayed victims alive. Later, we learn of his impotence, his fascination with the Marquis de Sade, and with books on abnormal psychology, theosophy, and the occult. In addition to Norman, all of the other major characters of the film appear in Bloch's novel (Mary [Marion], Sam, Lila, Arbogast) and many of the minor ones as well (Lowery, Cassidy, Sheriff Chambers). But there is no Caroline (the other secretary in the real-estate office), no menacing policeman, and, even though Mary trades her car three times rather than just once, no used-car salesman—all characters added by Hitchcock and Stefano who contribute to the irony and suspense of the film. Significantly, since most of the scenes in which Mother appears are filtered through Norman's point of view, Mother in Bloch's novel is an actual physical presence. Norman's point of view controls the narrative in most of the chapters in which he appears, and Mary's dominates in the two where she is featured; later we enter Sam's and Lila's points of view in chapters in which they are at the center of the narrative action, although Norman's point of view remains the most pervasive in the book. In fact, the novel is narrated chapter by chapter by these main characters from a limited-omniscient point of view.

When Bloch's clipped prose explores Norman's psyche, it occasionally becomes psychologically reductive. For example, when Mother berates Norman in the first chapter for his passivity and lack of "gumption" as he sits and drinks in the motel office, Bloch presents Norman's reaction in a manner that is explicit and judgmental: "He wanted to shout at her that she was wrong, but he couldn't. Because the things she was saying were the things he had taught himself, over and over again, all through the years. . . . Mothers are sometimes very overly possessive, but not all children allow themselves to be possessed. . . . It was really his fault as much as hers."[8] Later in the chapter, when she rebukes him for having talked "dirty" to her when he tried to explain "psychology," he responds pathetically that he was only attempting to describe "what they call the Oedipus situation" (17), a connection that Hitchcock and Stefano were able to project indirectly in the film. Throughout, Norman alternately condemns and justifies her behavior, while she by turns taunts and reassures him, becoming in the process the core of Norman's infantilized, murderous psyche.

In Bloch's narrative, Norman lives in a dark psychic netherworld symbolized by the swamp where he buries his victims and where in nightmares he dreams of sinking, first together with Mother and then alone (though this time he is saved by her). Everything about Norman and

Mother leads to the final two chapters, which serve as an explanatory coda to the narrative and complete his case history: the first, a detailed second-hand "psychiatric" analysis of Norman, his relationship with Mother, his crimes, and his motivation; the second, a final encounter with Norman, now, as in the film, totally transformed into Mother.

Mary, who becomes Marion in the film, is introduced during her eighteen-hour car ride to Fairvale, having already stolen the money from her employer. Bloch makes her a put-upon, bitter young woman of twenty-seven, who is more resentful than self-sacrificing. Having lost her father in her teens, been jilted by her boyfriend in her early twenties, and spent her adulthood supporting her younger sister and her ailing widowed mother, Mary's story is one of hard luck and pathos, and Bloch neither humanizes nor softens her: "The opportunity to go on to college had vanished, at seventeen, when Daddy was hit by a car. . . . [She] then settled down to support Mom and her kid sister, Lila. . . . The opportunity to marry disappeared at twenty-two, when Dale Belter was called up to serve his hitch in the army . . . and before long he began mentioning this girl in his letters. . . . Besides, Mom was pretty sick by then. It took her three years to die, while Lila was off at school" (22). The cynical tone of this reflective passage serves to harden Mary's image and to keep the reader at an emotional distance from her, as opposed to the empathy we feel for Marion in Stefano's script.

Desperate to marry, obsessed with aging and a sense that life is passing her by, she meets Sam Loomis on a cruise. Unlike the film, there is nothing overtly sexual about their relationship, and it is even implied that Sam has never seen her naked and that they are "waiting" until marriage. As in the film, his inherited debts prevent them from marrying, but there is no mention of an ex-wife, divorce, or alimony. The book's more hard-edged Mary assesses her life and her relationship with Sam and sees the stolen money as the means to her long-sought marriage. When she arrives at the motel with the stolen money, we know little of the actual relationship of Mary and Sam, but she is desperate and calculating. After recounting her unhappy history and Sam's situation, her resentment of her boss, Lowery, and of the rich oil man, Cassidy, becomes palpable, justifying the theft for her:

> . . . she watched old man Lowery make his steady five percent on every
> sale he made. She watched him buy up shaky mortgages and foreclose,

watched him make quick cunning cutthroat cash offers to desperate sellers and then turn around and make a fat profit on a fast, easy resale. People were always buying, always selling. All Lowery did was stand in the middle extracting a percentage from both parties. . . . He performed no other service to justify his existence. And yet he was rich. . . . .Mary hated him and a lot of the buyers and sellers he did business with, because they were rich, too. This Tommy Cassidy was one of the worst—a big operator, loaded with money from oil leases. . . . She'd never told Cassidy off, in public or in private [for offering her a hundred dollars for a weekend trip to Dallas]. . . . But she didn't forget. She couldn't forget the wet-lipped smile on his fat old face.

And she never forgot that this world belonged to the Tommy Cassidys. They owned the property and they set the prices. . . . *So* [she] *took the forty thousand dollars.* (27–28)

Mary views Lila through a similar prism of resentment as she contemplates her future with Sam and the forty thousand dollars: "Mary would have to be prepared to handle her sister, keep her quiet in front of Sam and the authorities. It shouldn't be too difficult—Lila owed her that much, for all the years Mary has worked to send her through school" (31). Mary is simply more deliberate and pragmatic than the more impulsive Marion that Stefano created, and she keeps an unwritten ledger of what is owed to her as she works out a scheme to get away with the theft and hide it from Sam and Lila.

There are moments in her encounter with Norman that parallel those in the film, but their impact upon her is not the same; unlike the film, there is little or no comic irony or profound insight. The scene in the novel that the film's parlor scene was based upon is different in tone and focus. In the novel it takes place in the kitchen of the house, not the motel parlor, and stays close to Mary's point of view and her reactions to Norman, who, as in the film, dominates the dialogue. Listening to Norman as she hungrily eats the supper of sausage, cheese, and homemade pickles he has prepared (as opposed to bread and butter for the film's more abstemious Marion), she is struck by his words, especially when, referring to Mother, he says as an afterthought to his tirade about sanity: "I think perhaps all of us go a little crazy at times" (a line Stefano used in the screenplay in slightly altered form). But unlike the perceptive, poetic Norman of the film, who speaks kindly to Marion as he laments the near-impossibility of individual growth or change, the more limited Norman of the novel confines his personal account to himself and Mother and to their relationship, particularly to the limitations Mother has imposed upon him: "I'm afraid Mother gets me a little upset sometimes. . . . I've never married. Mother was funny about those things. I—I've never even sat at a table with a girl like this before. . . . I tell myself that she'd be lost without me, now—maybe the real truth is that I'd be even more lost without *her*. . . . I don't smoke. . . . Mother doesn't approve of liquor in the house" (41–42).

Impelled to respond to this revelation, Mary asks Norman just what his mother allows him to do, whether he is "expected to act like a little boy all the rest of [his] life," and wouldn't it be better "if [he] arranged to put [Mother] in an—institution?" (43). This last suggestion enrages Norman, just as it does in the film, and brings him to his feet yelling: "*She's not crazy!*" And he takes full responsibility for Mother's behavior:

> "She's not crazy," he repeated. "No matter what you think, or anybody thinks. No matter what the books say, or what those doctors would say out at the asylum. I know all about that. They'd certify her in a hurry and lock her away if they could—all I'd have to do is give them the word. But I wouldn't because *I know,* and they don't know. They don't know how she took care of me all those years. . . . If she's a little odd now, it's my fault, I'm responsible. When she came to me that time, told me she wanted to get married again, I'm the one who stopped her, I was to blame for that! You don't have to tell me about jealousy and possessiveness—I was worse than she could ever be. Ten times crazier, if that's the word you want to use. They'd have locked me up in a minute if they knew the things I said and did, the way I carried on. . . . But who are you to say a person should be put away? *I think perhaps all of us go a little crazy at times.*" (44; italics added)

Realizing that he has gone too far, Norman admits to being bottled up and changes the subject, as Mary apologizes and leaves. Throughout their encounter, there is little to make Norman sympathetic or inspire identification with him: he is merely pathetic, angry, and strange. While what he says is more explicit, none of it has the insight and sensitivity of what the Norman of the film says at this moment. Even so, his final line resonates with Mary, becoming the very words that bring her to her senses and make her think practically:

Yes. It was true. All of us go a little crazy at times. Just as she'd gone crazy, yesterday afternoon when she saw that money on the desk.

And she'd been crazy ever since, she must have been crazy, to think she could get away with what she had planned. . . . Maybe she could manage to throw off the police. But Sam would ask questions. . . . And then there was Lila. (47)

While Mary recognizes how much more fortunate she is than Norman, her primary realization is how hard it will be to get away with the crime, and this is what makes her decide to return the money before the theft is discovered. Rather than reaching a moment of personal recognition and responsibility, as her counterpart does in the film, she reasons that it would be "crazy" of her to think she could make up some plausible explanation for her possession of the stolen money. Assured of her decision to return the money to the bank, and relieved and relaxed in her motel room before her fateful shower, Mary admires her body before a mirror. Unlike the more natural and unself-conscious Marion, she convinces herself of its sexual potential and even performs a kind of bump-and-grind: all of which, the reader learns in the subsequent chapter, Norman has witnessed through a peephole and is torn between arousal and revulsion. Her subsequent murder in the shower is much less a narrative centerpiece than it is in the film. It occupies five brief paragraphs and less than half a page and is presented partially from her point of view. It is more impersonal and matter-of-fact than terrifying: she sees the face of her murderer ("It was the face of a crazy old woman"), who, in contrast to the multiple stabbings in the film, cuts her head off abruptly with a butcher's knife.

Throughout the book, Bloch is not interested in reader identification with Mary, or with a transfer of identification or sympathy to Norman after her death, which are so central to the film. The impact that Bloch is interested in achieving does not depend on fully realized characters but on the narrative mystery that is unraveled at the end of the story: ultimately, Bloch aims to shock the reader with the book's final revelation. When Mary is killed, it is a moment of horror; however, we do not experience the sense of disbelief or loss that the film elicits with the death of Marion, with whom the audience has been encouraged to connect and whose depth and humanity have been "opened up," to use Evan Hunter's term. The book's emphasis is on the horror of the crime itself and the mystery of Norman/Mother, and to a lesser degree the mystery of Mary and her theft.

While the novel's revelation that Norman is Mother and the motivation for his crimes provides its shock ending, Mary's "true identity" becomes a subject of perplexity almost as soon as she disappears. For example, at one point Sam ruminates on how little he knew about the woman he was engaged to: "Sometimes he almost wondered if they hadn't made a mistake when they planned ahead. After all, what did they really know about each other? Aside from the companionship of the cruise and the two days Mary had spent here last year, they'd never been together. There were the letters, of course, but maybe they made things worse. Because in the letters, Sam had begun to find another Mary—a moody almost petulant personality, given to likes and dislikes so emphatic they were almost prejudices" (84). And later, as he and Lila try to make sense of Mary's disappearance and the missing money, he confesses: "I'm beginning to wonder how much any of us really knows about Mary. . . . I'm engaged to her. You lived with her. Neither of us could believe she'd take that money. And yet there's no other answer. She did take it" (163–64). The larger question of identity, the ultimate inscrutability and hidden lives of those we think we know, becomes a subtheme in the novel, linking Mary's transgression to Norman's acts of horror and situating them in the same continuum of psychological darkness.

None of the novel's characters possesses the poetic sensitivity of the film's Norman, or achieves the level of understanding or inspires the interest that Marion does. Arbogast, for example, enters into the narrative as a less prepossessing, more obvious, figure than his cinematic counterpart. A tall, slim, hard-nosed Texan in a ten-gallon hat, rather than the edgy urbanite created by Martin Balsam, who seems to have stepped out of a film noir, he appears in Sam Loomis's hardware store at the end of chapter 6 to interrupt the first meeting of Sam and Lila and dominates the discussion through chapter 7. After interacting with the two of them and proceeding to the motel, he is dispatched with a razor without much descriptive detail in chapter 9, in a manner as impersonal as the way Mary is killed: his death becomes almost an offstage action with little of the visceral horror it has in the film.

Interestingly, Sam Loomis in the novel, unlike the Sam of the film, accepts his lot in life without complaint, as well as the necessity to pay off his father's debts before he can start his own adulthood free and clear. A classical-music lover with a strong work ethic, he becomes a kind of rational touchstone for the theme of the unknowability and mystery of people, especially of Mary. Lila, however, takes a long time to believe her sister capable of the theft, and she prods Sam to investigate further at the motel, becoming increasingly impatient with his unwillingness to second-guess Sheriff Chambers's benign view of Norman and with what she considers Sam's small-town inertia and credulousness. Her relationship with Sam is more fully developed than Sam and Mary's and occupies much more of the novel.

The scene between Sam and Norman as Lila goes up to investigate the house elevates the novel's level of apprehension and suspense. After the couple discovers one of Mary's earrings in the bathroom of the cabin where she was murdered, Lila leaves to get Sheriff Chambers but decides to visit the house first, convinced that she will find Mary there. As Sam shares a drink with Norman in the motel office to stall for time, Norman, who has observed their discovery through the peephole, reveals to Sam that he removed Mother from her grave after she was buried because she wasn't dead, just in a state of "suspended animation." Then he knocks the alarmed Sam unconscious with the liquor bottle.

The subsequent chapter with Lila searching the house is the book's dramatic and tension-filled high point—and Bloch does not spare descriptive detail or adjectives. It certainly provided a model for Stefano and Hitchcock. Here, as in the film, Norman's world and history are uncovered in a manner that may have suggested to the director the book's potential for pure cinema. Narrated from Lila's point of view, the journey through the house is also a journey through Norman's personal pathology. On the second floor she discovers, in turn, a bathroom that belongs in "a museum exhibit," Norman's infantilized bedroom with his library of the occult and the pornographic, and Mother's elegant but bizarrely anachronistic Victorian bedroom with its four-poster bed, indented mattress, and pillow with telltale brown flecks: a room in which "she could feel a living presence." Then she proceeds down to the cellar and finally to the fruit cellar, which is the house's symbolic equivalent of the primordial burial swamp where Norman disposed of the bodies. There, her encounter with the mummified corpse of Mrs. Bates and then with Norman, descending the staircase dressed as "Norma," screaming and brandishing a kitchen knife, provides the book's most terrifying moment and is virtually replicated in the film.

The final two chapters present the psychiatric explanation and then, as in the film, Norman alone in a barred room totally transformed into

Mother, ruminating about events and responsibility for them. But in the novel the psychiatrist's explanation is conveyed second-hand through Sam to Lila: he serves as a filter for the more technical and abstruse ideas, and she as a stand-in for the reader. It is a more detailed and, in some ways, more persuasive account than the one in the film, lacking the sweeping, reductive glibness of Simon Oakland's explanation. Beginning with an account of the dredging of the swamp for bodies, it is an attempt to read Norman's criminally insane mind in terms of 1950s psychology. According to Sam, the psychiatrist traced the genesis of Norman's psychosis back to his suffocating relationship with Mother and his crimes to his reaction to the shock at the discovery of Mother and her lover in bed. This discovery drove him to poison them with strychnine—the first of his murders—and led him to his new dual identity as Norman/Mother, an identity first revealed in the "suicide" note he wrote for her to cover his crime. Sam recounts the psychiatrist's explanation: "'Apparently, now that [her murder] was all over, [Norman] couldn't stand the loss of his mother. He wanted her back. As he wrote the note in her handwriting, addressed to himself, he literally *changed* his mind. And Norman, or part of him, *became* his mother'" (216). Through spiritualism and the "preservative powers of taxidermy," he deluded himself into believing that he kept her alive, and whenever a crisis arose, such as the arrival of a woman who aroused his sexual desire, Mother as "Norma" Bates possessed him and resolved it: "'Afterward he'd hide her image away, because in his mind she was the real murderer and had to be protected'" (218).

After listening carefully to Sam, Lila is grateful for the explanation of why her sister was murdered and even has a measure of compassion for Norman, as she begins to share the earlier view of sanity that her sister had heard Norman articulate: "'Right now, I can't even hate Bates for what he did. He must have suffered more than any of us. In a way I can almost understand. We're all not quite as sane as we pretend to be'" (219).

The brief final chapter presents Norman totally metamorphosed into Mother, now speaking in her own voice, as Bloch refers to Norman with the pronoun "she" and has him adopt her point of view, adding visceral reality and eeriness to the psychiatric explanation. "Mother" is confident in her calm and serenity, convinced that she had no part in the murders that "a bad man" tried to blame on her, murders she can remember because she had "been there at the time, watching. But all she did was watch" (222). Mother is also certain that "to be the only one, and to know that you are real—that's sanity, isn't it?" (223). And the novel ends with the fly, as in the film, and Bloch's final line of Mother's self-exoneration, "Why, she wouldn't even harm a fly" (223).

The Birds

"It's not only here, it's everywhere. . . .
Something has happened to the birds."
—Daphne du Maurier, "The Birds"

Like *Psycho, The Birds* was influenced by *Alfred Hitchcock Presents.* Science fiction—especially the supernatural borders of that genre—had become a standard source for the television show. In addition, several of the show's scripts were based on Daphne du Maurier stories. "The Birds" was as close as she ever came to writing science fiction, and the story had the kind of disturbing scenes of birds attacking humans and a dark ending that the best of the *Alfred Hitchcock Presents* programs featured (relieved, of course, by the wry Hitchcock codas). Here, however, there would be no superficially benign appearance of the director to offset the apocalyptic fears the film would arouse. But unlike *Psycho, The Birds* would be given the big-budget, color treatment of the major Hitchcock films of the 1950s, with characters added and relationships expanded.

"The Birds" was the third work by Daphne du Maurier that Hitchcock used as a source and the one he adapted, or transformed, the most thoroughly in a strictly narrative sense. As Evan Hunter remarked, at the outset of their collaboration he and Hitchcock decided "to throw out everything besides the bird attacks."[9] According to Hunter, Hitchcock decided to take from the story only the motif of a menacing natural force beyond human control, which provided the element of shock that he wanted to achieve, particularly after the success of *Psycho.*

The du Maurier story is set on the Cornwall coast of Britain in a remote farm community where rapidly increasing bird attacks isolate a poor family. The birds kill almost everyone in their path, leaving the whole nation ravaged by the end. The transfer of the story's somber English postwar setting to the more picturesque and sunny America of the film's contemporary period accounts in part for the differences between the two works. The tone of the du Maurier story is far darker, more pessimistic, and more global. However, a close reading shows that while much was changed, particularly its setting, characters, and tone, more was kept than has been recognized. Much of this is not in the Hunter screenplay but in the film itself and appears to be the result of Hitchcock's own choices and additions to the script as a director. Whether he would have acknowledged it or not, the visual background and atmosphere in the literary work as well as specific narrative moments found their way into his film.

Du Maurier was one of the twentieth century's masters of suspense and the macabre, and "The Birds" is a richer, more polished, and more accomplished literary work than Bloch's *Psycho*: its cultural background, or moment, was the contemporary apocalyptic fear of the cold war rather than the popular psychology that influenced Bloch. First published in 1952, the story follows the pattern of many of du Maurier's tales by presenting an inscrutable terror that threatens her characters—here, murderous birds intent on destroying them and, by extension, human civilization. Essentially a short story without an extended and complex narrative, it offered the director and scenarist Hunter a single dramatic direction and an increasing arc of suspense. Written with close attention to visual detail and a compact narrative, it engages the reader with its terrifying fable as it builds suspense. Taking place in late autumn, the narrative is filtered through the limited omniscient point of view and consciousness of Nat Hocken, a partially disabled farmhand who was wounded in the Second World War. He lives in a remote agricultural part of the English coast with his wife, young daughter, and son in a simple stone cottage that has no telephone or electricity.

The film's point of view was transferred predominantly to Melanie Daniels; much of what we see is from her perspective. But unlike the film, in the story we learn little about the narrator, his family, the farmer that he works for, the farmer's wife, or their other hired man. All of them play roles in the narrative, but no individual tensions or shortcomings in relationships are presented or suggested. Unlike many of du Maurier's other works, this story is not about character interaction; there is no sense, as in the film, of people coming together, or growing, or loving in the face of adversity. It is simply about terror and survival, and the characters' efforts to stay alive as the mounting horror of the birds is presented in visceral, visual terms.

To understand the relationship between story and film, it is necessary to begin with the differences between Hitchcock and du Maurier. Her short story is more explicitly a work of horror, more about nature being out of control and bent on destroying humankind than about "character." As such, it is centered on the near-universal destruction perpetrated by the birds and the physical rather than psychological reactions to them. While the human characters are sketchy at best, her birds are more prominently characterized, even distinguished, as to different sizes and species, particularly by the narrator. If there is a psychological level to the work, it is about the psychology of isolation and survival, of living under the most horrendous assault, increasingly cut off from an outside world that itself is being destroyed. It has the texture of an early cold-war fable, with the family's final hopeless claustrophobic seclusion in their home becoming a metaphor for the postnuclear isolation of final survivors. In terms of tone and irony, there is no light comedy such as appears in the first sequence of the film, where Hunter made an attempt at screwball comedy, and no style, glamour, romance, or love in the world she creates, with its limited humanity: everything about the life of Nat Hocken and his family is stark and austere. Their home appears adequate to shelter them, but it is a tight, sparse cottage. They have no "gramophone" for entertainment, and their battery-operated "wireless" is their only contact with the outside world. London is mentioned, but unlike San Francisco in the film, it is not associated with urbanity, sophistication, or artificiality, and, unlike Mitch and the Brenners, the Hockens never seem to go there. There is a town nearby, but in contrast to Bodega Bay, it never appears. In every way, the immediate locale of the story is more rural, agricultural, remote, and secluded. Its larger setting is a postwar world with the Hockens' part of it characterized by scarcity, hoarding, and physical deprivation, as was the experience of many in England after the war.

The story begins on December 3, when the weather has made an abrupt turn to winter cold. Nat, "a solitary figure" who likes "best to work alone," observes "great flocks" of birds of every variety flying inland: "Black and white, jackdaw and gull," and "sea birds too," all of them appearing more agitated "and restless than ever."[10] At first he attributes their restlessness to the coming "hard winter" and sudden cold, which the locals speculate, with cold-war overtones, may have come with winds originating in Russia. But later, as he tries to shut a window in his bedroom, a bird flies through, pecks his hand, and draws blood, then six strike his face, and in the next room a gathering of "robins, finches, sparrows, blue tits, larks and brambling birds" (157) attacks his children. At first, Nat rationalizes that the birds are seeking shelter from the cold and that the frigid wind has driven them to attack, "as though a madness seized them" (158). Trying not to be alarmed, he takes comfort in the physical security provided by the ordinary everyday reality of "the cups and saucers, neatly stacked upon the dresser [a possible parallel to the broken but neatly hung cups and saucers that Lydia sees at Dan Fawcett's farm in the film], the tables and chairs, his wife's roll of knitting on her basket chair, the children's toys in a corner cupboard" (158–59). But soon he realizes how dire the situation is, and he begins to take measures to fortify his house and protect his family.

When Nat travels to the farmhouse to inform the farmer and his wife about the peril of the birds, they are skeptical and dismissive; even after the attacks intensify, they refuse to take them seriously. Nat, however, understands how extreme the danger is and characterizes the assaults in military terms, comparing them to "air-raids in the war" and the birds to an organized army waiting upon "some signal" or "order" (161, 169) to attack again: an army that attacks in sequence from the smallest sparrows to the largest birds of prey. He discovers that they time their attacks in conjunction with the tides, with six-hour intervals between them—intervals he uses for securing his house with boards, nails, and fencing wire. So while Nat takes precautions and closes up windows and chimneys, sealing his family in, the farmer refuses to see how dire things are and jauntily goes off with a rifle to kill birds, as if to a "shooting match" (170). But when the wireless reveals that all England is under siege, Nat takes comfort that he has tried to protect his family, rationalizing it as a matter of absolute individual rather than community responsibility, which is a motif in the film: "Each householder must look after his own" (166), he asserts, as he abandons hope of convincing or helping others. Accordingly, the family's growing isolation and the lack of a sustaining community become obvious, and Nat's self-reliant resolve is seconded by the official voice on the wireless. Moreover, the official responses prove hopeless, as military counterattacks with fighter planes are futile and even suicidal. Masses of birds fly into the aircraft, and Nat curses "the inefficiency of the authorities" (189) as he hears the sounds of the distant planes crashing into the sea.

Before the story comes to its inconclusive but foreboding ending, Nat and his family make a last desperate trip for supplies to the farm, where he discovers a postapocalyptic landscape and the ravaged bodies of the farmer, his wife, and the hired man, all of whom had refused to heed his warnings. After returning home with whatever food and provisions they can scavenge, the Hockens experience bird attacks upon their cottage that become more relentless and intense. During a lull, Nat tacks up heavier boards, even barbed wire, realizing that most of the surrounding houses have been devastated and that there are few, if any, survivors in their neighborhood and perhaps the whole nation. The BBC is no longer broadcasting on the wireless, and they are unable to get stations from other countries as the instrument soon grows silent. Their sense of foreboding increases, and Nat's wife desperately hopes that "'surely America will do something'"—a plea with obvious postwar and cold-war resonance. As the story ends, Nat and his family are sequestered on the ground floor of the cottage (a prototypical bomb shelter); he switches on the silent wireless, smokes his last cigarette, and listens "to the tearing sound of splintering wood, and wonder[s] how many million years of memory were stored in those little brains, behind the stabbing beaks, the piercing eyes, now giving them this instinct to destroy mankind with all the deft precision of machines" (192).

The dark, seemingly hopeless tone of this ending contrasts with the ambiguous conclusion of the film: the Brenners and Melanie give up their refuge, leave their scenic coastal home, and drive to San Francisco, where the bird attacks have not yet reached. The Hockens, in the limited way they are characterized, bear little similarity to the more privileged, affluent, and positive-minded Brenners. Hitchcock and Hunter transformed the austere English family of a cold-war fable into a full-blown bourgeois American family. There is no equivalent to Melanie here, just as there is no Annie and no family dynamics to speak of. The birds bring out no particular tensions or shortcomings among them, as individuals or as a family, and while the Hockens' resolve is admirable, they do not seem to grow emotionally or spiritually as a result of the attacks, as happens in the film. Nat's admonition, "'We've got to depend upon ourselves'" (184)—as close to a psychological message as the story conveys—could also serve as a lesson in the film, albeit an inadequate and hopeless one in the story. Nat's individual determination and resourcefulness in the face of catastrophe define his character, and while Mitch also possesses these qualities in the film, his ability to grow, bond with, reassure, protect, and, most significantly, love the other characters marks him as more complex and interesting than Nat.

Unlike the film, the du Maurier story does not strongly suggest that in order to survive, families and communities must bond and work together, rather than remain as isolated individuals. There is no presentation of the larger community, as in the Tides Restaurant scene, beyond the incidental depiction of the farm people, and no moment of self-sacrifice as is exhibited by Annie Hayward when she gives up her life to save Cathy's. As the story ends, we do not know how long the Hockens will prevail, but we realize that their days are numbered, which is not a forgone conclusion in the film for Melanie and the Brenners, all of whom may not only survive but even prosper as a result of the way extreme adversity has brought them together.

Despite these differences between the two narratives, there are affinities—many of them visual—that shed light on what drew Hitchcock to the story and how he used it. Some of the descriptions in du Maurier's text bear comparison to similar moments in the film, and several of these were added by the director after Hunter submitted his final draft of the screenplay. In the story, the first bird attack on Nat, during which his hand is cut, is reminiscent of the early gull attack on Melanie's forehead as she returns to Bodega Bay by boat from the Brenners' home; it was added by Hunter and Hitchcock late in preproduction. Both attacks are sudden, almost imperceptibly swift, with the birds quickly drawing blood and disappearing. In the story, Nat goes to the window and opens it, "and as he did so something brushed his hand, jabbing at his knuckles, grazing the skin. Then he saw the flutter of the wings and it was gone, over the roof, behind the cottage. . . . The bird had drawn blood" (156). In neither work do we learn what the birds' motivation is—they simply act.

The scene of the birds coming down the chimney in the film, as Hunter acknowledged, was taken explicitly from the book and replicated in the screenplay. In the story, Nat realizes that the "birds were coming down the chimney, squeezing their way down" it (180), but this scene occurs later in the narrative, when the situation has already begun to look hopeless, not in the early uncertain stages, as in the film. To the next sequence in the film Hitchcock added the terrifying image of Lydia discovering Dan Fawcett's bird-ravaged corpse on his bedroom floor, his legs first coming into her point of view.[11] This echoes the scene late in the short story where Nat discovers the bodies of the farmer and his wife: "[The farmer's] body was close to the telephone. . . . The receiver was hanging loose, the instrument torn from the wall. . . . She [was] upstairs. . . . He could see her legs, protruding from the open bedroom door. Beside her were the bodies of the black-backed gulls" (187). Even the attack on the schoolchildren in the film, which has generally been regarded as an original addition in the screenplay, has a partial parallel in the story when Nat's daughter climbs off a school bus with several other children who run home across the fields as gulls circle overhead while he carries her to safety. Hitchcock and Hunter elaborated these scenes, and Hitchcock gave them specific visual shape, adding a fully developed bird attack upon the running children.

The final sequences of the film also bear comparison to similar visual moments in the book. The final attack on the house—a scene Hitchcock added during production when he improvised, as he told Truffaut,[12] because he was insecure about the screenplay—is suggested in the book as well. Toward the end of the film, when Melanie and the Brenners are isolated in the house, the birds' assault becomes so intense that their beaks peck through window shutters and doors and bloody Mitch's hand when he tries to keep them from getting through. Mitch fortifies the house by nailing wooden planks over the windows and leaning an antique mirrored chair against the front door. In the book, Nat nails boards over the windows in the same way and later adds metal and barbed wire as additional fortification. Further, in the penultimate scene, the Hockens are under a siege very reminiscent of the film as they hear "the sound of splintering wood, the talons tearing at the wood" (183). As Nat tries to secure things, he realizes that something alarming has happened, something that in the film makes possible its most terrifying scene, the assault upon Melanie: "Nat looked about him, seeing what furniture he could destroy to fortify the door. The windows were safe because of the dresser. He was not certain because of the door. He went upstairs, but when he reached the landing he paused and listened. . . . The birds had broken through" (183).

When Melanie goes upstairs in the film, the visually climactic moment occurs as the birds break through into the house and attack her. This moment in the story parallels the film and is also foreshadowed earlier during the birds' first assault on the Hockens' cottage when they attack the children in their bedroom. Nat immediately comes to their aid in a manner that is reminiscent of Mitch's rescue of Melanie: "[S]tumbling into their room, he felt the beating of wings about him in the darkness. The window was wide open. Through it came the birds . . . swerving in mid-flight, turning to the children in their beds. . . . He felt the thud of bodies, heard the fluttering of wings, but they were not yet defeated, for again and again they returned to the assault, jabbing his hands, his head, the little stabbing beaks sharp as a pointed fork. . . . and then in greater darkness [he] beat at the birds with his bare hands" (157). The visual similarity here indicates that Hitchcock was influenced by du Maurier's narrative, just as he was by a passage in the book that precedes the Hockens' visit to the farm where Nat discovers the dead bodies. As Nat and his family leave their house for the last time in the early morning darkness, the birds are everywhere: "Nat saw them, on the hedge-rows, on the soil, crowded into the trees, outside in the field, line upon line of birds, all still, doing nothing" (185). This scene compares to the film's final inconclusive tableau in which the ubiquitous birds are in similar positions as the Brenners drive off and disappear into the distance. Thus while the book lacks the film's central characters and the psychological melodrama acted out among them, elements of the story's mood and atmosphere, and some specific visual details, were effectively translated by the director into key moments of the film's visual narrative.

What he did not follow in du Maurier were specific lines, scenes, and background radio broadcasts that would have provided explicit cold-war references and allegory, even though an examination of Hunter's evolving screenplay reveals that the writer had initially included them in the narrative.

Marnie

"It's all exciting really . . . building up
a new history, making a new person."
—Winston Graham, *Marnie*

Winston Graham's novel *Marnie* (1961) was certainly not a typical source for *Alfred Hitchcock Presents.* The novel's psychological explorations would never have fit the short-story format of the television show, and its length and detail necessitated deciding not what to add to the complex narrative, but what to keep. What drew Hitchcock to this project, however, was his desire to pursue sexual material that he would have been forced to avoid up to this moment in Hollywood history. The passionate dramas of Tennessee Williams had been made into films, and the social-realism films of the 1950s had opened new subject matter to filmmakers. In addition, the triumph of television forced Hollywood to expand its appeal to younger audiences in order to compete and survive, as Hitchcock had done with *Psycho*. Graham's novel was about the intersection of sexuality and criminality, and Hitchcock was confident he could use it to film more daring sexual and violent images than his audience was accustomed to. The "rape" scene in the novel was its daring moment that the director wanted to bring to the screen: it certainly did make audiences squirm, but it also cost him a screenwriter.

Graham's novel, the most detailed and complex of the three sources and the one that presented the most problematic adaptation, is also a kind of psychological case study. Graham, a successful English novelist who wrote the popular Poldark series, based *Marnie* on a composite recollection of two women from his youth: one was a compulsive bather whose mother had warned her never to have dealings with men; the other was a married mother of three who, like Marnie's mother, had had multiple sexual encounters with men during the war and whose daughter became a compulsive thief. Like Bloch in his portrayal of Norman Bates, Graham brought contemporary popular Freudianism and psychology to bear in creating Marnie. Although he had never been in analysis, according to Tony Moral, Graham claimed to have been influenced by his reading of the English psychiatrist Charles Berg's *Deep Analysis* (1947), an account of a psychotic patient's analysis and transformation from a sexually dysfunctional and impotent schizophrenic into a highly successful and functioning man. Graham had also consulted a psychologist to learn about the behavior and habits of women thieves. The resulting novel *Marnie* was well received in Britain and was published in the United States the same year to positive reviews, the *New York Times* calling it a "phenomenally successful use of a woman's viewpoint, and a rare and happy balance of psychoanalytic and novelistic method."[13]

Hitchcock bought the rights to *Marnie* the year it was published, immediately recognizing the potential of the convergence of Marnie's sexual problems and her criminality and of Mark's attraction to and relationship with her. It provided the more extreme kind of material he was looking for at the same time as it stayed within the bounds of the traditional melodrama he had made many times before.

In the novel, Graham introduces us to Marnie long after she has become a compulsive thief and just at the beginning of the events that will change her life and propel her finally on the path from sickness to health. But the author is more interested in identifying and describing the beginning of a cure for his protagonist's psychological dilemma—her inability to feel love more than just the inability to make love, as in Hitchcock's film. Since she resists any change with all her considerable intellect and will power, the "thrills" in the novel consist of the dramatic events that break down her self-imposed walls of isolation and false identities and force her to confront her own self and her need for others. The long arc of this process makes the narrative more detailed and complex than Bloch's more limited and focused storyline in *Psycho* or du Maurier's more compact story structure in "The Birds." But the heroine's severe neurosis and the moments of high drama and suspense placed it in the same category of literary intensity for the director.

Graham's use of first-person narration would seem to reduce all mystery and suspense, as we have total access to Marnie's thoughts and feelings and learn everything that happens to her and all the book's revelations through her own words. Yet we learn early on that Marnie is a mystery to herself, that she does not understand why she is compelled to carry out her well-planned robberies of the companies she works for, and that she has no desire to determine the reasons. She has become comfortable with her shifting identities: Mollie Jeffrey, Marion Holland, Peggy Nicholson, Mary Taylor, the pseudonyms she chooses at each of the businesses she robs, are all just as real—and just as unreal—as Marnie Edgar, her ostensible self. A change of hair color creates a new person without any true history. Only when she visits her mother and her mother's companion, Lucy Nye, at Torquay (the English seaside town where they live) does she resume her role as Marnie, the dutiful daughter of a lame and proper religious woman of fifty-six, but even in this familial context she is living a lie. She has told her mother that she works as a well-paid secretary for the wealthy Mr. Pemberton, who takes her along on expensive trips abroad and pays her well, which accounts for her long absences and her many presents for her mother when she makes her periodic visits home. It is only when she stays at a hotel called the Old Crown near Garrod's Farm, where she keeps her horse, Forio, that Marnie feels a genuine emotional life. But such an isolated, ascetic life does not allow Marnie any access to the unconscious feelings that have caused her to despise sex, to adopt a perpetually hard-boiled attitude toward human life, and, of course, to live the life of a criminal.

When she takes a job at John Rutland and Company, planning to continue her pattern of working efficiently until she understands the company's operations and then to abscond with all the money she can, she meets two men who fall for her, both directors of the firm: Mark Rutland and his cousin, Terry Holbrook, who was replaced in the screenplay by Lil. As she is wooed by the serious, well-mannered Mark and the cunning, man-about-town Terry, Marnie keeps a complete emotional distance from both of them, though she strives to maintain friendly but somewhat impersonal relations until she has the opportunity to carry out her thievery. She robs the safe, deposits the money in various banks under various assumed names, returns to Garrod's Farm and Forio—and is traced there and caught by Mark Rutland. Here is a significant difference between the novel and the film: unlike the Mark in the novel, the film's Mark is a controlling, manipulative figure with a fetishistic interest in Marnie, as opposed to the firm but usually mild-mannered character Graham created, who falls deeply in love with Marnie almost immediately upon her coming to work at his firm, and not because she is an interesting specimen that he has captured.

Mark, a widower for two years, restores the stolen money to his firm at the same time that he tries to understand what drove this beautiful young woman to become a thief. Marnie tells some of the truth about her life but hides much of it (her mother, her previous thefts) in an attempt to keep him at bay. She even lies about being afraid of her developing feelings for him and deciding to run away rather than get involved in a mismatched relationship between a gentleman and what she calls a "back-street urchin."[14] But this false revelation of an emotional attachment to Mark backfires: he decides to marry her because he is in love with her and to cover up her crime. Marnie is trapped, so against all her instincts, she becomes engaged to marry Mark Rutland as a way of avoiding going to prison and now has to face a new dimension of her "sham life [that] didn't include Marnie Elmer" (156), one over which she has limited or no control.

During their honeymoon, all her disgust with sex is forced to the surface of her being. In response, Mark presents her with a realistic yet tolerant and even-minded approach to lovemaking: "'The physical act of love is a normal outcome of the emotional state of being in love. Surely . . . Of course, without emotion there is only sex. But without sex there is only sentimentality. Between a man and a woman the two elements of love become one'" (162). When Marnie retorts that "'[i]t's . . . animal,'" Mark responds, "'We *are* animal—in part. We can't take our feet out of the mud. If we try we fall slap on our faces. It's only by accepting our humanity that we can make the most of it'" (162). When, soon after, she tells him that she doesn't love him, that she pretended to have feelings for him so he wouldn't send her to prison, Mark describes love with an impatient parody of St. Paul: "'Love isn't always blind. . . . Nor is it always patient. Nor is it always kind'" (173), just before he forces himself on his horrified wife. The next day she unsuccessfully attempts to drown herself while swimming.

Though her attempt fails, in a sense she succeeds in killing her old, illusory self, for this episode begins the second half of the novel in which, reluctantly, Marnie is forced to begin to know herself and to forge a true identity. Mark bribes her into going to see a psychiatrist, Dr. Roman, by promising that he will bring her horse Forio to their home. At first, Marnie gives the doctor "the same mixture of truth and make-up that [she had] given Mark" (204) and has no intention of revealing her repressions to him—or. indeed, to herself. In their second session he does convince her to free-associate with the word "sex": "'Masculine and feminine. Adjectives end in *euse* instead of *eux.* Male and female . . . Adam and Eve. And Pinch-me. Dirty boys. I'll slap your bloody face if you come near me again'" (134). In their next session, when Roman presses her on the subject of sex, she clams up and pretends to fall asleep. Clearly, the doctor has uncovered major resistances that indicate a severe sexual neurosis—yet, unlike a strict Freudian, he sees the sexual disgust as a symptom of a larger emotional malaise.

This is where the novel differs significantly from the film: first of all, Roman, the psychiatrist, has been removed from the film's plot, as has Mark's rival, Terry Holbrook. As a result, Sean Connery's Mark has to play amateur psychiatrist as well as conflicted lover to fill in the gap Roman has left, and the rival becomes Lil, who is vying with Marnie for Mark's affection, as opposed to the two men/one woman situation in the novel. Secondly, the book's deepest issue is not sex but instead the human feelings that are involved in eros and all other relationships; as Dr. Roman tells her, "'I suspect a good deal of the time you live in a sort of glass case, not knowing real enthusiasm or genuine emotion; or feeling them perhaps at second hand, feeling them sometimes because you think you ought to, not because you really do'" (220–21). The therapy sessions begin to open a channel to her unconscious life, where all her genuine emotions have been hidden, and this process continues until the end of the novel. When she again visits her mother—unbeknownst to Mark, of course—Marnie begins to confront her with questions about her childhood, especially about her father's death when she was six. Clearly, Roman's questions about her past have induced her to recover it.

The next major change in Marnie is when Roman's questions about a strange childhood memory of a tapping at her window and an accompanying feeling of cold cause her to break down and cry. Disturbed by painful feelings, Marnie skips her next therapy sessions and agrees to resume therapy only after an unexpected and frightening incident: at a dinner party she attends with Mark, a Mr. Strutt appears who met Marnie on several occasions when she was masquerading as Marion Holland at a branch office of his firm in Birmingham—an office that she robbed before she had come to work for Rutland's. Strutt insists that he has met her, but Marnie denies it, and Mark covers for her. However, Strutt privately tells Mark about the robbery in Birmingham, so her husband now knows that Rutland's is not the first firm Marnie has stolen from. Later that night, Mark demands that she tell him about all her past robberies; reluctantly, she finally does and agrees to resume therapy to please the man who can so easily decide her fate and send her to prison.

Again, her free-associations bring her back to the repressed memory of her father's death, and again she breaks down: "I felt such a fool crying there because I'd remembered something I'd forgotten and because I felt again the twist of grief inside me, remembering that day and how I knew I'd never have complete protection or shelter or love again" (270). When an ex–chief constable, a friend of Mark's, comes to the house to advise him how to deal with Marnie's past crimes, Marnie overhears the conversation and feels betrayed by her husband. She decides to run away from him and her current life, so when she next visits Roman she makes up dreams and memories and happily resists any of his attempts to break through her lies: the psychological progress she has made is interrupted by her sudden decision to flee to France.

Three major events stop her from trying to escape. First, on a fox hunt with Mark and other acquaintances, Marnie is appalled by the gleeful attitude of the people in the hunting party toward the killing of defenseless animals, and has another onrush of emotion: "They hadn't any real feelings at all. . . . I think I was *feeling* more just then than I'd ever felt before in my life. . . . It was happening terribly to me" (308). This overwhelming emotion causes her to let Forio take her away from the hunt at top speed, pursued by Mark, only to end in a horrible spill over a large hedge when Mark is badly injured. Mark is hospitalized, and Forio is destroyed on the spot: "I went home, and bubbles of pain and grief and sheer hurt kept rising and bursting in my heart" (315). Consciously, this trauma has not shaken Marnie's decision to flee the country, even when she visits Mark in the hospital and he talks about their making a new start. Then the second unexpected event happens: when she goes to rob the safe at Rutland's before she flees to Paris, Marnie suddenly discovers that she really has changed and is consciously aware that, though she can leave her husband, she cannot go through with this theft while he is in the hospital. She feels awful doing so, but she puts the money back.

The third event that keeps her in England is the shocking discovery that her mother has died—and subsequently the more shocking discovery that when Marnie was a child her mother had killed her baby, Marnie's brother, because he was fathered by one of the sailors she had been sleeping with while her husband was away at sea. The movie substitutes a repressed memory of Marnie's own act of murderous violence as the cause of her neurosis for the shocking discovery in the novel, though it retains the context of her mother's promiscuity. Neither is a satisfactory explanation from a psychoanalytic viewpoint, but the novel's revelation certainly presents Marnie as more of a victim of her mother's psychosis and subsequent denial. Shortly after this discovery, Marnie finds herself feeling compassion for a young boy who also has just lost his mother, and in this genuine feeling of empathy she breaks out of her alienation as she realizes that "maybe everybody's griefs aren't that much different after all. I thought, there's only one loneliness, and that's the loneliness of all the world" (372).

So Marnie's neurosis is not cured by the recovery of a repressed traumatic memory, as in the film, and her disgust with sex may or may not be lessened. However, she finally feels pity for her mother, not anger for raising her to be disgusted by the erotic life—clearly her mother did so because the terrible killing of her child had ultimately been caused by her inability to control her sexual desires. And though at the very end of the novel she is betrayed by Terry, Mark's rival in business and for her, and is presumably headed to prison, she begins to think of the possibility of real love between her and Mark in the future. And so the novel concludes not with her "cure" but with her decision not to run away and assume yet another new identity, and with her ability, as Marnie Elmer, to feel the genuine human emotions she has lived without before her relationship with Mark Rutland—certainly a prerequisite for a cure.

The style of Marnie's first-person narration in the novel is colloquial, unsentimental, and direct—much like that of the Angry Young Man novels and plays of the fifties written by authors such as Allan Silitoe and John Osborne. She is a working-class character who indulges in some social climbing as she robs her way though the English middle class, and her attitude toward her social superiors is usually a combination of surface respect and inward condescension—in her mind, they are never as clever or resourceful as she. In the film, class issues are at once more complex and fluid, as Marnie easily passes for more than the adult slum child she once was throughout the period of her criminality, and in the end seems to journey seamlessly from the bottom of the Baltimore's lower class to the upper ranks of Philadelphia's main line. In the novel, social class is presented more explicitly than it is in the film, both in relation to Marnie's childhood and to the world she inhabits as an adult woman, and economic issues play a more significant role in general. In the film, the adult Marnie's relationship to her childhood home and neighborhood seems tenuous at best, and her poverty is never singled out. Although we are presented intermittently with Marnie's mother's shabby house and the mean street that runs in front of it, Marnie herself never seems even remotely working-class, roots that would presumably surface at least part of the time. (Based on the novel's depiction of Marnie, it is difficult to understand why Hitchcock always assumed that Grace Kelly would be effective in this role.) Tippi Hedren's Marnie projects class and at least nascent sophistication, and we never glimpse the tough-minded, self-confident, proletarian attitudes behind this projection that the Marnie of the novel constantly reveals in her first-person description of her thoughts and emotions. By contrast, the childhood of the novel's Marnie is presented against a backdrop of postwar deprivation in a distressed urban working-class neighborhood with more cruelty than community. Unlike the much-discussed mythic and expressionistic locale of Mrs. Edgar's Baltimore dockside row house in the film, Marnie's primal neighborhood of origin in the book is a hard place, harboring painful memories for her that highlight her low social stature. As an adult, Marnie in the novel is more visibly hard-edged and canny, as her origins would seem to dictate, than the gentler, vulnerable thief of the film, and she conveys a sense that she has both stolen and clawed her way up to her present position.

Similarly, the Rutland family in the book, including Mark, is more middle-class and businesslike than the faux-British gentry in the film; they own a printing firm rather than the more tony publishing house of the film. Mark's family is represented by his plump, cheerful, and tolerant English Mum rather than the patrician "Dad" of the film, with his tweeds, waistcoat, and gamekeeper. In the novel, the character that was replaced by Lil, Mark's male cousin Terry, has a palpably cunning and cutthroat quality about him, and Marnie is a worthy adversary for him at the card games he presides over. By contrast, Lil, while competitive with Marnie for the attention and affection of Mark, conveys a sense of breeding and noblesse oblige that is absent in her graceless, grubbing, male novelistic counterpart. Significantly, too, the novel's Mark Rutland seems more aggressive as a businessman than he is as a lover/possessor of Marnie.

The film does add dimensions to the story that Graham did not include, and some of them are compelling. Hitchcock's expressionistic techniques, particularly the red suffusions and eerie flashbacks, convey Marnie's psychological disturbance with a visceral effect that is lacking in the novel because Marnie, as first-person narrator, has built up so many defenses against her past that she rarely allows memories to disturb her present activities. This happens only during the later therapy sessions with Dr. Roman, when the free associations he asks her to make unlock disturbing feelings against Marnie's will. In the film, her panicky reactions to the color red begin early and culminate in the storm that breaks the windows in Mark's office and result in her clinging to him for emotional support. The storm bothers her in the book (though the scene takes place at Mark's home), but not to the point that she needs physical contact with her employer. By the end of the storm scene in the film, we are convinced that Marnie's compulsive thievery is the result of whatever repressed memory has caused such deeply neurotic symptoms as her deep-seated fear of redness.

Interestingly, of the three sources, only the literary one for *Marnie,* the Graham novel, has a female protagonist, yet all three films have a woman as the central figure in their narratives. Clearly, in the case of the novel *Marnie,* Hitchcock was interested in the contradictions the female character presented, her combination of beauty and intelligence, on the one hand, and her thievery and revulsion from men, on the other hand—elements he retained and explored in the film. For *Psycho* and *The Birds,* where there were no such female characters in the source, he and the writers either expanded the role of a minor female character or refashioned the narrative so that a woman would be at its core. In *Psycho,* he and Stefano greatly expanded and developed the role of Mary/Marion, making her the center of the narrative for the first third of the film and her death the unsolved mystery for the rest of it; in *The Birds,* he and Hunter substituted Melanie for Nat as the central consciousness of the narrative and connected the bird attacks to her life and relationships, which they also constructed. All three women protagonists are attractive but marginal people within the worlds they inhabit. Each is deeply flawed and vulnerable in her own way and desperate for emotional security and stability: the issue that the director and the writer made the plot of the film turn upon. Each is an appropriate character around whom they fashioned the film's psychological motifs and built audience identification. Thus, from source material that suggested but did not stress the plight of young, single women in the late 1950s and early 1960s, Hitchcock and his writers created a triptych of films that do exactly that, in powerful and innovative ways.

The director and Joseph Stefano. Courtesy of Marilyn Stefano.

Joseph Stefano in 2002. Courtesy of Amy Srebnick.

Evan Hunter in the 1960s. Courtesy of Drajica Hunter

Evan Hunter in his seventies. Courtesy of Drajica Hunter

Jay Presson Allen in the 1960s. Courtesy of Brooke Allen.

Jay Presson Allen circa 2000. Courtesy of Brooke Allen

Janet Leigh and John Gavin in the opening hotel scene of Psycho. Courtesy of Jerry Ohlinger, with permission of the Hitchcock trust.

Hitchcock directing Janet Leigh in Marion's bedroom. Courtesy of Jerry Ohlinger, with permission of the Hitchcock trust.

The chimney attack in The Birds. *Courtesy of Jerry Ohlinger, with permission of the Hitchcock trust.*

The Brenners flee the momentarily passive birds. Courtesy of Jerry Ohlinger, with permission of the Hitchcock trust.

The director and Tippi Hedren at Rutland's. Courtesy of Jerry Ohlinger, with permission of the Hitchcock trust.

Marnie in her riding clothes. Courtesy of Jerry Ohlinger,
with permission of the Hitchcock trust

CHAPTER 3

From Treatment to Script

The question of Hitchcock's involvement in creating the plot and text of his scripts is a complex one, as we have seen. He worked closely with the screenwriter in adapting the source and developing the story and characters, and then at a certain point he would ask the writer to go home and produce a first draft. When this was submitted, Hitchcock again took complete control. He would direct the writer as to what needed to be cut and what needed to be added in the subsequent drafts as he worked toward the creation of a shooting script. Finally, he would normally ask the writer to assist him as he broke the penultimate draft down into shots. For Hitchcock, the most important phase of this creation process was the first one: "After all, the most enjoyable part of making a picture is in that little office, with the writer, when we are discussing the story-lines and what we're going to put on the screen, searching for freshness and so forth."[1]

But the collaboration continued all the way to production: "I do not let the writer go off on his own and just write a script that I will interpret. I stay involved with him and get him involved in the direction of the picture. So he becomes more than a writer; he becomes part maker of the picture."[2] Clearly, it can be seen the other way around as well: Hitchcock was not only the director, but, as indicated above, he was part writer of his films. Even his choice of genre was determined by his assessment of his own abilities as a writer: "I choose crime stories because that is the kind of story I can write, or help to write, myself."[3]

When the first draft was submitted, a new stage in the process began: the revisions that would culminate in a shooting script. A study of the various drafts of the three films under consideration reveals the director's three distinct objectives as he monitored them: (1) the removal of what he called "no scene" scenes; (2) the addition of some strongly visual shots or the elaboration of a scene to provide increased insight into a character, usually without new dialogue; (3) and the removal of dialogue that did not add anything substantial to characterization or merely indicated some idea that the camera had already conveyed. Between the first draft and the shooting script, the screenplay would often be rewritten substantially at least three times, as the collaboration between the director and his writers continued. At the same time, Hitchcock began to work with his preproduction team to scout locations, design sets, and assess technical requirements, work that would often influence later drafts of the script.

Psycho

Psycho is in many ways the most successful example of a collaboration between Hitchcock and his screenwriter late in his career. Yet the first adaptation of the novel for the director was not done by Stefano but by James P. Cavanaugh, and this draft was submitted in June 1959. Cavanaugh had written scripts for television and several for *Alfred Hitchcock Presents.* Although the script he produced stayed closer to the book than Stefano's, some of the important character developments that appear in the film began with him. Interestingly, like Stefano's later drafts, Cavanaugh's script begins with Mary Crane and follows her until she reaches the Bates Motel. His Norman, while still an alcoholic like the character in the novel, is a shyer, gentler, more sympathetic figure and anticipates the Norman of the film. Although he has little of the poetic articulateness of the film's Norman, he still has lines that are reminiscent of him, such as when he tells Mary, "I wonder if it's ever really possible to get away from the past." And Cavanaugh's initial character descriptions indicate Norman's psychological link to Mary when his directions specify that their unhappiness can be seen in their eyes. As in Stefano's script, Norman has a conversation with Mary over supper that inspires her to resolve to return the stolen money. What they talk about, however, focuses more on their finances than the "traps" of their personal lives and in that sense is closer to the way they are characterized in the novel: Cavanaugh's Norman is at "the end of the road," as the motel is about to go bankrupt and be repossessed, while Mary claims to have just inherited money and thanks him for "stopping her from making a terrible mistake." But this version of the crucial parlor scene lacks the depth of characterization, psychological insight, and tension of the Stefano script and the finished film, and at its end Norman even makes a pass at Mary.

As in the novel, Cavanaugh's Mother is more of an actual presence than she is in the film, and her angry, distorted face is seen for fleeting moments in his script. A straight razor is used to kill Mary and later Arbogast, not a kitchen knife, and after the shower murder Norman exclaims, "Oh my God—Mother—What have you done—What have you done!"—lines that come very close to what he says in Stefano's script and the film. He cleans up after the murder, and there is also a scene of a briefly hesitating car descending into the swamp, with an added melodramatic touch of the money popping out of Mary's purse in the back seat. In the next sequence, Arbogast appears at Sam's hardware store after Lila and plays essentially the same investigatory role he does in the film. Yet even though he confronts and accuses Sam and then Norman, he generates little of the anxiety and suspense of the character in the film. As Cavanaugh's Arbogast enters the house to interview Mrs. Bates, Norman can be heard admonishing her in the background. After descending the stairs, "smiling grotesquely," Mother attacks and kills the detective at the landing. Afterwards, there is a scene of Norman disposing of Arbogast's car in the swamp that parallels the earlier one. When Lila later goes down into the cellar, Norman locks her in there, and she encounters not the mummified skeleton of Mrs. Bates but a dummy version of her. Norman then enters, menacingly dressed as Mother, but Sam comes from behind and knocks him unconscious. The script concludes with Norman in a jail cell and the sheriff giving the final explanation of things, rather than the film's psychiatrist, as Mary's car is towed out of the swamp.

Significantly, the roles and relationships of Mary, Sam, and Lila are different in the Cavanaugh script than they are in the film. As in the novel, there is no postcoital scene with Mary and Sam at the beginning. Sam does not appear in this early script until after her murder—and Mary is a far less interesting and attractive character than the Marion of the film. She is thirty-four and frustrated, and it is her age, her history of broken engagements, and her unhappiness that cause her to steal the money, much like the Mary of the novel. She is described by her sister Lila as kind and self-sacrificing, but also as someone who always tried too hard to be "perfect" and as a result became "rigid and unbending" and "snapped." In fact, Lila becomes a more attractive substitute for the rigid Mary in the second half of the Cavanaugh script. She and Sam not only solve the murders but also become a couple in the process, a more appealing and attractive one than Sam and Mary. This screenplay emphasizes their growing relationship, one that promises the possibility of a more conventional, and perhaps consoling, coda to the ending of the story, especially when they embrace as Sam tells Lila that he loves her.

As Stephen Rebello points out in his study of the making of *Psycho,* many of the sequences that Hitchcock and Stefano later created to build up tension before the murder already appear in fledgling form in Cavanaugh's text.[4] Mary's long car ride, as she flees with the forty thousand dollars, is here, as is her trading in her car for a different one. But her ride lacks the ominous tension that appears in Stefano's script and the film, and the scene with the used-car dealer involves simply a quick transaction with none of the ironic suspense of the film and could be classified as a "no scene" scene that merely moves the plot along. Significantly, there is no highway patrolman to menace Mary in her car as she absconds with the money. Further, in the second part of Cavanaugh's screenplay, neither Norman nor the couple being formed by Sam and Lila generates enough interest to compensate for Mary's absence. Unlike Stefano's script, there is little psychological nuance in the characters Cavanaugh creates, little ironic humor in the dialogue, and too few signature visual moments. Yet, working together with Cavanaugh, Hitchcock had begun the process of crafting the narrative verbally and visually, a narrative that would take definitive cinematic shape in his collaboration with Joseph Stefano.

Though Hitchcock never showed Stefano Cavanaugh's script when they began working together in September 1959, they followed Cavanaugh in starting the film with Mary, who soon became Marion. But the hotel tryst with which Stefano begins his screenplay sets the tone for the remainder of the movie: one that is dark, furtive, frustrating. In addition, he dramatically transformed the characters of Mary and Norman that Cavanaugh and Hitchcock had sketched out, making them two people who are interesting in themselves and not merely stock types in a crime drama. Stefano worked on the script throughout the fall of 1959, and the draft he considered his final one is dated November 10, 1959; some small additional changes were made afterwards throughout November and into early December. The draft before this, dated October 19, is the draft that Stefano completed before he went over it scene by scene with the director. On some day between October 19 and November 10, then, Hitchcock invited Stefano to his home to assist him with breaking down the writer's final draft into shots.

Stefano recalled this fascinating process in some detail and remembered how specifically visual it was: "We went through the script all that day, and he would say, 'I want a big face here.' The Assistant Director [Hilton Green] did drawings for some of the shots. Hitchcock made the decisions about camera movement. He knew how it would look. But precise shot details were not done for all the sequences. For example, he would not write, 'Shot of M. Crane in bra. Cut to close up of the money. Then back to her.' But it was all in his mind, whether he wrote it in or not. He saw everything, as if his vision was the audience's vision. He was seeing it for you. And now all he had to do was go on the set and make sure that people did what they were supposed to do."[5] Like the original October script, the November 10 version is set up in "master scenes," with each scene in a new location being assigned a specific number.

The changes made to Stefano's dialogue in the first draft were relatively minor. Rarely did Hitchcock have a collaborator who shared his sense of humor so fully and whose working methods dovetailed with those of the director so smoothly. Lines Stefano had given to Sam in the opening scene about the two of them being "a working man" and a "working girl" and their problems being "a regular working-class tragedy," which played up their desperation in terms of their financial struggles and social class, were eliminated, as was his reference to their relationship and trysts being "tax-deductible." Also eliminated were lines that used words such as "crime," "criminal," and "conscience," which foreshadowed too obviously the crime-and-guilt motif. In a number of scenes Stefano bracketed dialogue that seemed long, and though Hitchcock shot these exchanges, he cut most of them in the editing room. Other lines were cut for various reasons. For example, in the first scene of the original script, but not in the finished film, Sam refers to a "private island," a phrase used later by Marion in her fatal encounter with Norman. Stefano revealed that this was one of the lines that John Gavin couldn't say effectively, so it was cut.[6] In the scene in the real-estate office, when Marion says that she is going to spend the weekend in bed because of stress, Cassidy comments in Stefano's first draft that bed is "the only playground that beats Las Vegas,"[7] a line cut at the urging of the censor. (Hitchcock occasionally instructed his writers to leave certain provocative lines in the script so that later, by agreeing to cut them, the director could save other more significant lines in his compromise with the censor.) Cassidy also refers to his prospective son-in-law in this script as a "penniless punk," and

Caroline, the other secretary in the office, played by Pat Hitchcock, is described in this draft as being in her late teens rather than a woman in her thirties. Hitchcock also cut a line of Mother's after Norman has carried her down to the cellar, when she compliments him for "handling [the situation] like a man," as it seemed to be at odds with her resistance to being put there and relates more clearly to Bloch's Norman than to the one Stefano and Hitchcock had created.

Most of the changes that appear in the November script, however, are visual. In the scene in Mary's bedroom, several camera indicators have been added: it now "lowers," "shoots across," and "retreats" to follow Mary. When Mary encounters Lowery on the street as she is driving out of town, several point-of-view shots have been added that contribute much tension to the scene. In the used-car-dealer scene, a number of new shots have been added of the car lot and the patrolman across the street, some of them from Mary's point of view. Also, specific shots have been added during the voiceovers while Mary is driving in the rain, and now we see the "large old house" behind the motel specifically from Mary's point of view. Perhaps most significantly, a close-up of "the Various Birds" is added to the parlor scene. In the November script, there is an "extreme high angle" of "Mother" coming out of her bedroom to kill the private detective, and a "BIG HEAD" of Arbogast immediately following as he registers shock and horror at being stabbed. It was the writer himself who insisted on the high-angle shot (Hitchcock at first objected that such a set-up would be too costly), as well as on a shot during Lila's approach to the big house at the end of the film in which the motel is clearly seen in the background, reminding the audience that Norman is supposedly behind her in one of the cabins and that the events in the house and in the motel are always linked. In both cases, Stefano convinced Hitchcock that these shots were necessary to keep the audience from guessing too much.

Raymond Durgnat points out in his study of the film that the screenplay is essentially laid out in master scenes that sometimes "specify a particular angle or effect," and he suggests that it often seems as if "Hitchcock's mind's eye had storyboarded" everything.[8] Yet the final shooting script of November 10, while it contains many more delineated shots than does the October script, still does not break the entire film down into separate shots. The additions were made primarily to visual scenes that contain little dialogue. Thus, *Psycho* is also a fascinating test case in relation to Hitchcock's oft-repeated claim that all the creative work for him was done before the cast and crew arrived on the set, that he wished he didn't have to actually shoot the film once it was already preplanned with the writer down to the final editing. The myth surrounding these boasts is that every shot we see on the screen was either storyboarded or at least indicated in the shooting script. *Psycho* reveals that the process was actually a combination of various approaches to the "decoupage" (the shot-by-shot progression of the film): some scenes were broken down shot-by-shot in the final script (usually ones with little dialogue), some were storyboarded in conjunction with the cinematographer—and some were devised during the shooting process, though the director may have already had many of these "new" shots more or less clear in his mind before the filming began. As a rule, even in the case of Hunter's and Allen's screenplays, which contain many more individual shots than Stefano's, a scene in the completed film contains more shots than does the corresponding scene in the shooting script.

For example, the shot/reverse shot pattern used during the crucial conversation between Marion and Norman is not indicated at all in Stefano's script. In fact, all their dialogue here is listed under Number 103: "MEDIUM CLOSE SHOT—MARY," even though in the finished film the camera cuts back and forth between Marion and Norman. Again, this may be because Hitchcock knew he would later storyboard this scene with his assistant director. (Not all written or drawn preplanning is still extant; Hilton Green told us that the parlor scene between Marion and Norman in *Psycho* was storyboarded by Joe Hurley, the production designer, for example, but the boards have not been preserved. And Saul Bass, as Rebello and others have pointed out, storyboarded the shower scene.) But each scene was certainly shot with the final cut clearly in the director's vision at all times. Again, Green supported the idea that Hitchcock knew during shooting what a scene would look like on the screen when he said that during some scenes the director would stop the action in the middle of two actors' dialogue because he knew that the remainder of the scene would be shown from a different angle and distance. As Green put it, "He cut in the camera a lot."[9]

Were even the camera movements preplanned? In 1970, Hitchcock explained that "you don't necessarily storyboard all of those, because it's very hard to do camera movements. Your artist usually draws a big arrow, which really doesn't convey where the camera is going. I think you more or less have to leave that till you go on the set. But you have it in mind."[10]

This attests once again to the fact that what could be preplanned was, even if the design did not exist in the writer's screenplay or an artist's drawing but only in Hitchcock's mind. So the myth is grounded in truth.

As far as the cutting room was concerned, its only important function for Hitchcock was to shorten the preplanned shots, if necessary: "every piece of film is designed to perform a function. So therefore, literally, the only type of editing I do is to tighten up. . . . But actual creative work in the cutting, for me, is nonexistent, because it is designed ahead of time—precut, which it should be."[11]

Based on a comparison of the October and November scripts, Hitchcock, always concerned about audience reaction and involvement, had also asked Stefano to rewrite the scene when Sam and Lila first meet in Sam's hardware store. Hitchcock cut Stefano's later scene in which Sam and Lila discuss how Marion was always prepared for self-sacrifice and helping others, which echoed the Cavanaugh script, because "he felt it wasn't moving the story."[12] In the second half of the film, Hitchcock resisted Stefano's efforts, as he had with Cavanaugh's, to develop a more intimate relationship between Sam and his dead lover's sister than Bloch had included in his novel, preferring that the audience focus on Norman's relationship to his "mother," the murderer: in Stefano's psychiatrist scene, Sam and Lila would stand in for the audience in its desire to know why "Mother" had killed Marion and whether Norman would be able to protect her from retribution. (Certainly Hitchcock was right with regard to viewers seeing the film for the first time; however, on repeated viewings, some critics have argued, the audience's knowledge of who "Mother" is leads to a slackness in the second half that a more interesting Sam/Lila relationship would have compensated for.)

Interestingly, the November 10 draft, for all intents and purposes the shooting script, contains a stage direction written by Stefano that suggests his commitment to the darker issues the film explores. At the end of the psychiatrist's explanation, the script reads: "Lila begins to weep softly for Mary, for Arbogast, for Norman, for all of the destroyed human beings of this world." This scene did not make it into the film, but it certainly reflects the fact that, despite its neo-Gothic trappings, Stefano intended *Psycho* to contain universally tragic implications—a conception that Hitchcock did not want to be articulated so explicitly.

The November 10 script also eliminated or altered significant details from the October script. For example, in the earlier version, Mary is so tired before she pulls off the road that she "almost swipes an oncoming car." In addition, the patrolman who questions her in the morning is "young, bright-faced, handsome"—much different than the suspicious officer of the shooting script. In the October script, the used-car salesman is also more genial and trusting than his later counterpart. Referring to his business, he says, "Darned if we won't keep it friendly and trusting in spite of everybody! That's how the world ought to be, friendly and trusting in spite of everybody"—lines removed by November 10. (Were they too obviously thematic for the director, picking up a line of Lowery's voiceover during Marion's car ride about trusting somebody who works for you for ten years?)

Once Mary reaches her fatal destination, a number of interesting small details have changed from the October to November scripts. During the parlor scene, when Norman tells Mary that his mother is ill, she replies that his mother sounded "lusty," a word changed, for the better, to "strong" in the final script. And after Norman talks about "our own private traps," Mary says, as she does in the November 10 script, "Sometimes we deliberately step into those traps," but this time adding, "That's called making a 'lifelong mistake'"—an unnecessary and too obviously thematic comment for the director, unless Stefano was suggesting the irony that Mary's life would not be very long because of the trap she had stepped into.

Other key changes from the October 19 script involve the second half of the film: some of these are verbal, some visual. In the October 19 draft, at the hardware store Sam responds to Lila's interrogation about Mary's whereabouts with lines that harken back to the film's opening tryst: "What do you think, we eloped or something? Or we're living in sin?" In the same draft, Arbogast is stabbed in the chest, not in the head. When Lila speaks of her sister, she is unable to make sense of her theft and emphasizes Marion's sacrifice for her when she was young and the fact that she "always tried to be proper." Later, at the sheriff's home, a stage direction has Sam "put his arms around [Lila] comfortingly." And, perhaps most significantly, the psychiatrist's scene is not in this script. It was added to the November 10 script mostly on Stefano's insistence that the audience needed a final rational explanation for the story's bizarre events.

One stage direction in the first draft that met with resistance, this time from Anthony Perkins, accompanied one of his most famous lines in the film, "A boy's best friend is his mother." Stefano had added that Norman says this "with gallows humor," but, as he told us, he later learned that "actors don't like cues." In the film Norman says the line without apparent irony or insight into its Freudian implications.

The overall effect of the changes Hitchcock and Stefano made to the October 19 script that became embodied in the shooting script is that the entire first half of the film has now become much more subjective, as the added shots, particularly the numerous new point-of-view shots, either directly or in the rearview mirror of her car, put the viewer much more clearly into the mind of Mary/Marion. In essence, verbal motifs have been replaced by visual ones, and the most suspenseful moments of the script are now characterized by their use of the camera ("big heads," a close-up on the stuffed birds, specific camera movements in her bedroom as she considers whether to steal the money). And in many cases the new visuals substitute for reduced dialogue: Mary/Marion is now characterized as much by what she looks at, and reacts to, as by what she says.

The Birds

The Birds, in contrast to *Psycho,* provides the clearest example of how insufficient communication between Hitchcock and his writer could affect the outcome of a film, especially when the director was not satisfied with the story or characters. Although Hunter met with Hitchcock for the customary early weeks of discussion between writer and director, he soon went off to his rented house in Brentwood to do the actual writing, and the two did not communicate sufficiently during this period. As a result, during the revision process, when Hunter had left for New York and was working mostly from there while Hitchcock was in Los Angeles, their ability to understand the other's ideas and intentions for the script was compromised, and the director, who had a different conception of the narrative, made substantial revisions to what Hunter wrote. The extent of the revisions reveals how insecure the director was with the screenplay, and he continued to make changes well into production.

Hunter's first draft was submitted in November 1961. The entire scenario is arranged by shot, not by scene, which is the normal procedure for a screenwriter. Hunter wrote it that way without discussing it first with Hitchcock. The director ultimately ignored much of Hunter's shot breakdown but did not discourage the writer from presenting future drafts in this format, presumably because he liked the fact that Hunter was thinking visually while constructing the narrative.

Hitchcock took extremely detailed notes about this first draft, most of his proposed changes finding their way into later drafts, and he sent his observations in a letter to Hunter dated November 30. First of all, Hitchcock asked Hunter to cut entire scenes. In the first draft, the opening pet-shop scene is followed by a scene at Melanie's father's newspaper office in which she talks to her father and her friend Charlie, one of his employees, about trying to track down Mitch so she can continue her practical joke. In the finished film that scene is condensed into a phone call Melanie makes to Charlie as she watches Mitch's car pull away from the pet shop. Next, when Melanie arrives in Bodega Bay, Hunter had written several scenes that were subsequently dropped: she goes to a general store to buy a toothbrush, pajamas, a suitcase, and so on, and then tries to check into a hotel but learns that it has no vacancies. Finally, she arrives at Annie's home.

Later in the script, Hitchcock asked Hunter to cut a church scene in which the minister is reading the "all is vanity" lines from Ecclesiastes, and Melanie again encounters Mitch. Although it linked the impending bird attacks to misdirected human energy and pride and provided atmosphere, the scene was cut because it too obviously contained a message for the director and did not move the story forward. In addition, Hitchcock cut a scene of a town meeting in which the frightened civic leaders of Bodega Bay discuss what they can do about the increasingly violent bird attacks. The town meeting was eventually replaced by the Tides Restaurant scene.

The office scene, the general-store scene, the hotel scene, the church scene, and the town-meeting scene were cut because Hitchcock considered them to be "no scene" scenes, whereas Hunter had originally included them to flesh out the details and associations of the story. He also cut a later scene of Melanie and Mitch joking with one another about the motivation behind the bird uprisings, at the end of which they embrace. Even the opening pet-shop scene barely survived. Hitchcock wrote to Hunter that such a scene "might have narrative value but in itself is undramatic. It very obviously lacks shape and it doesn't within itself have a climax as a scene on a stage might."[13] He kept it, though, presumably because it established the "screwball comedy" tone that Hunter had suggested for the first part of the film and which he hoped would keep the audience off guard, an idea that Hitchcock liked. Hunter made these changes immediately, and they were incorporated into the next draft, which is dated December 14, 1961.

Hitchcock also asked Hunter to add incidents early in the script that let the audience know that "the birds is coming," as in the publicity mantra. So Hunter added the attack of the gull on Melanie in the boat, and Hitchcock himself suggested the dead bird that lands with a thud at Annie's door to foreshadow the terrible violence to come. (Interestingly, in *Me and Hitch* and during our interviews, Hunter maintained that he and Hitchcock should have included more bird attacks.)

Two days later (December 16), Hitchcock added all of Melanie's point-of-view shots to the scene in the script of the attack upon the town of Bodega Bay when the man carelessly lights the gasoline with his discarded match. Even the man's offhanded ignorance of the consequences of his action could be seen as reinforcing the idea of human "complacency," which Hitchcock alleged was one of the unspoken themes of the film despite Hunter's later assertion that this was an afterthought on the director's part. In any case, this is a particularly good example of how Hitchcock would add nonverbal scenes to the writer's scenario. And most dramatically, he handwrote ideas on small notebook paper for the progression of shots in the crow sequence, notes that we were able to examine at the Herrick Library and that were later storyboarded and inserted into the script.

Hunter originally wanted to make the protagonist a young female schoolteacher who comes to Bodega Bay shortly before the bird attacks begin. But by the time he began the actual writing of the first draft, she had become the playgirl Melanie Daniels. The teacher idea survived in the film in Annie Hayward, the most important of the secondary characters in the film. In the first meeting between Melanie and Annie, Hunter had included dialogue that Hitchcock wanted either cut or rewritten. Much of it was intended to present an image of Bodega Bay as a more authentic and genuine place to live and work than the urban San Francisco. For example, in the first draft Annie has an interesting speech about how Bodega Bay is "real . . . with all its fish smell from the canneries." She also explains that she came to Bodega Bay because this "reality" contrasted with San Francisco's "phoniness": at an evening in "a beatnik joint," her date said, "Annie, I love to watch you drink cappuccino." Teaching school in the small town is altogether more meaningful for Annie: "I'm *doing* something here, Melanie," she insists.

All this was cut, presumably because the lines added nothing substantial to Melanie's characterization and were expository, not dramatic.

Also, the dialogue given to Annie that the director cut seems to be left over from an earlier conception of the film in which the protagonist was the schoolteacher. The lines are inappropriate for a secondary character, which Annie's schoolteacher has become, though some of the San Francisco/Bodega Bay polarity—superficial sophistication versus small-town authenticity—is transferred later to Melanie's character. Hunter replaced these lines with ones that hinted at Annie's past relationship with Mitch—and his mother—lines that increase the dramatic tension of the scene because of Annie's suspicion that this attractive, sophisticated blonde may very well be, or at least become, Mitch's new love interest. Clearly, these changes removed the possibility that Hitchcock could consider this a "non-scene" because of a lack of conflict.

As he did with *Psycho,* Hitchcock immediately began to revise the script by adding more point-of-view shots for the protagonist, in this case Melanie, as he continued to stress the subjective approach to telling his story. But in the case of *The Birds,* Hitchcock's major goal in the revision process was to add depth to the characterization, in particular to dramatize more clearly the changes in Melanie's attitudes and values, and not only to flesh out the plot. This was a new challenge for the director, because for the most part he left these matters to his writers. When the film suddenly veered from comedy to horror, Hitchcock intended the audience to experience a shock similar to that which was felt by the original viewers of *Psycho* when Marion is, without warning, brutally murdered. But the director wanted the characters' depth to grow accordingly, and he was dissatisfied with the character development in Hunter's first draft. Hunter had attempted to give the dramatic situation allegorical and political significance with allusions to the cold war in the dialogue and background and references to the Bible. But the director wanted a deepening of the personality conflicts and changes instead. In addition, a number of people on his staff who had read the script insisted on knowing why the birds were attacking humans, and Hitchcock wanted Hunter to consider providing an explanation. And, much more important for the director himself, he also told Hunter, "One final thought that has been bothering me for some time: Have we really related the whole of the bird invasion to our central characters?"[14]

Hunter responded by writing a new scene in December in which Mitch and Melanie discuss possible reasons for the bird uprising, first humorously and then seriously. They speculate that one of the birds is the leader who tells the others, "Birds of the world unite. You've nothing to lose but your feathers." Then their mood darkens, the speculation becomes more dire, and the scene ends with them turning to each other and kissing "suddenly and fiercely" to overcome their fear. Presumably Hitchcock was not in favor of the joking revolutionary reference, and he resisted such an attempt to make the developing romance the primary relationship among the characters. Instead, he was searching for visual and verbal signs of family and community, not exclusively the erotic connection between men and women.

Hunter's script also had Annie originally go up in the attic in the film's penultimate scene, only to be nearly killed by the marauding birds. Instead, she is killed off during an earlier bird attack protecting Cathy. Probably, again, this choice stemmed from Hunter's first idea for the film—that the protagonist would be a schoolteacher—and also from his desire to deepen Annie's character, but in this second draft it is appropriately Melanie who undergoes the attic ordeal. Thus the complexity of Annie's character was sacrificed to develop Melanie's latent courage, her growing willingness to confront danger to protect others. Yet it also suggests how much the screenplay and characterization were in flux.

Hitchcock sent Hunter notes on this latest draft that impelled him to continue developing characterization and addressing possible reasons for the bird attacks. Hunter's third draft, completed in January 1962, includes a discussion between Melanie and Annie about the possibility of oedipal problems involving Mitch and Lydia and, more importantly, a new scene in the Tides Restaurant in which many of the townspeople propose possible explanations for the birds' destructiveness—what Hunter always felt was the best-written scene to be preserved in the final film despite Hitchcock's negative comments about it to Truffaut.

Thus Hunter agreed with Hitchcock that it would be best for the movie if no particular reason were established for the attacks beyond an inexplicable defect in nature, including human nature. In dialogue dropped near the end of the finished film, Cathy asks Mitch why the birds are trying to kill people, and Mitch responds, "I wish I could tell you. But if I could answer that, then maybe I could also tell you why people are trying to kill people."[15] This idea that humans must first stop their own self-destruction is reinforced in the first draft by a radio announcement after the initial Bodega Bay attacks that the Common Market is considering a treaty whose "adoption would mark an important step towards European unity." This is replaced in the January 1963 draft by a State of the Union address by

President John F. Kennedy that proclaims "the goal of a peaceful world of free and independent states." Hunter's references gave the screenplay a spectrum of human relationships, from the couple to the family to the community to the world, all of which are being threatened by the birds. This suggests that the birds' violence reflects the need for tolerance, community, and peace in the conflicted human community of 1961.

Hitchcock removed these radio broadcasts because he eschewed politics as basically uninteresting to the audience, and possibly because he felt that such speeches were more appropriate for one of his espionage films, though the influence of these ideas remained in the script through their cultural resonance. He seems to have agreed with Hunter that no specific explanation for the bird attacks should be given, whether scientific or philosophical, but he disagreed with the writer that the script should explicitly refer to the contemporary world situation—in other words, the cold war—as a condition for the birds' destructiveness. Again, Hitchcock instead wanted the characters' relationships to be deepened.

Hunter insisted to us that he and Hitchcock never discussed "meaning," though the director did indicate in his November 1961 letter to Hunter that "I'm still wondering whether anything of a thematic nature should go into the script," a statement that seems at variance with his earlier avoidance of such connections. He added scoffingly, "I'm sure we are going to be asked again and again, especially by the morons, 'Why are they doing it?'"[16] This ambivalence of writer and director toward "theme," however, must not be viewed as a reluctance to make a serious film. "Meaning" or "significance" in any Hitchcock film arises out of character development and plot situation; it is never imposed from without by a conceptual scheme. What Hitchcock was reluctant to provide in the case of *The Birds* was social, political, or even spiritual ideology, though this seems to have been Hunter's original inclination. The movie is "about" the effects of the bird attacks on the characters themselves. When Hitchcock wondered whether the story of the characters was sufficiently related to the attacks, he meant that psychologically there should have been a logical progression of the main characters' emotional intensity and awareness as the attacks become more and more vicious—not that the attacks "represent" some aspect of the characters' psyches or that they somehow prompt the attacks to occur.

With *Psycho,* Hitchcock was never uncertain about the essential characterization in Joe Stefano's first draft. But in the case of *The Birds,* even as he began the momentous preproduction process for the film's panoply of special effects, he still asked his old friends and collaborators Hume Cronyn and V. S. Pritchett to comment on the characterization in the January 1962 screenplay, and both agreed that Melanie's character in particular was underdeveloped. In April Hitchcock wrote to Pritchett, asking him to rewrite the "dune" scene. The new dialogue included a reference by Melanie to her being abandoned by her mother for a hotel man from the East when she was twelve.[17] These new lines particularly upset Hunter. No one involved in the film seemed to have known who actually wrote them; in 1999 Tippi Hedren told us that she supposed Hitch and Alma had written them during production. Yet an extant handwritten letter from Pritchett to Hitchcock at the Herrick Library, dated April 12, 1962, which contains the dialogue from the scene, proves that it was he who wrote them just before filming began.[18]

Thus, as late as April Hitchcock was still trying to add complexity and motivation to Melanie's character. In Hunter's first draft, after the first major bird attack, one stage direction reads, "This is not the Melanie we saw at the beginning of the picture. Her hair is disarrayed, and her face and clothing are streaked with soot. But beyond a surface physical appearance, there is a weary wisdom in her eyes, and strength in her as she stands looking toward the distant smoldering town."[19] This image was never shot, but here is where Hunter's and Hitchcock's visions for the film coalesced: Hitchcock never stopped striving to convey Melanie's external and internal transformations through the revisions he asked from Evan Hunter and his own subtractions and additions to the screenplay. Significantly, none of these subtractions or additions involved the bird attacks: all involved deepening or clarifying characterization, which was also the goal of the director's constant use of the subjective camera to visualize Hunter's scenario.

One of the obvious difficulties that Hunter and Hitchcock had in this regard is that the characters in the original Daphne du Maurier story had been discarded. The director and writer were creating new fictional characterizations and not adapting earlier ones, as had Joseph Stefano and Jay Presson Allen. This challenge had been present in the case of earlier successful Hitchcock films, when he worked with writers such as Thornton Wilder (*Shadow of a Doubt*) and Ben Hecht (*Notorious*), but here the necessary empathy between collaborators when they are creating characters was intermittent. Increasingly Hitchcock turned to other writers who were personal friends. Hunter was miffed by this and felt undermined by Hitchcock. He did not seem to be aware that this was not unusual for Hitchcock: throughout his career sometimes two or even three writers were involved in drafting a script.

One particularly interesting aspect of the different drafts that is less prominent in the final shooting script is the treatment of the lovebirds. Evan Hunter told us that the lovebirds were his idea and that they originated from the screwball-comedy concept for the early scenes in the film. He then proceeded to use them as symbols of the development of the relationships among the principal characters. Originally, they are the basis of Melanie's attempted practical joke on Mitch and the ostensible reason for her trip to Bodega Bay (to bring them as a gift to Cathy). After their first intimate conversation during the dune scene in Hunter's first draft, in which Melanie implicitly suggests to Mitch that she is defensive about the value of her lifestyle, they return to the Brenner house to find that the lovebirds in their cage are "tweeting madly"—obviously a sign of the developing love between Mitch and Melanie. Later, just before their first passionate kiss in the scene that never made the final film, there is a close shot of Melanie and the lovebirds in which she smiles, pokes her finger into the cage, and imitates the birds' friendly tweeting. Clearly, Hunter was using the lovebirds as an index of Melanie's openness to this new relationship and Mitch's growing affection for her.

As the first draft progresses, the significance of the lovebirds is extended to include all the love relationships among the characters, not only the romantic one, and to encompass a kind of love that would extend to family and community. Cathy in particular sees them in this light. When Mitch speculates that it is natural for birds to flock together, even in such destructiveness as has now become frighteningly evident, Cathy turns her head toward the lovebirds and says, "Not all of them." Mitch himself is not certain about the nature of the lovebirds. Several pages later, just before the last big bird attack, Hunter included a close shot of the lovebirds watching Mitch and wrote in a stage direction: "Is there menace or innocence in their eyes? He cannot tell." A few shots later, Hunter wrote, "Again, it is impossible to read their expression. Malice or benevolence? He raises his hand, brings it towards the birds in the cage. . . . As he thrusts in through the bars, the birds sit unmoving. One of them tweets." Mitch feeds them, and "then, tweeting, they begin to eat." This shot is immediately followed by lights suddenly going out, and the growing erotic love relationship between Mitch and Melanie is again foregrounded: "In the near darkness we see them embrace and kiss."

Finally, in the first draft's final scene, the car with all the main characters speeds through the ravaged town as the birds attack. Lydia, fearful of them, has insisted that the lovebirds be put in the trunk after Cathy has brought them from the house. Cathy asks Mitch during their hectic dash towards freedom, "Do you think they're all right? In the trunk? Can they breathe?" Mitch answers with "the faintest smile," "I think they're all right, honey." Mitch, too, has obviously come to see the lovebirds as an omen of hope, as a sign of the benevolence in nature, again including human nature, and the hope that love will survive and protect them despite the overwhelming evidence of evil and destructiveness.[20]

Though these shots were later cut, Cathy's intuitive understanding of the lovebirds' nature is retained. In his conversation with Truffaut, Hitchcock comments that "that little couple of lovebirds lends an optimistic note to the theme,"[21] though the interviewer himself seems to see the lovebirds as serving an ironic purpose. Hitchcock insists that the lovebirds are introduced in the film's first scene because "love is going to survive the whole ordeal."[22] In fact, Hunter's final script has Mitch saying at the end: "What do we have to know? We're all together, we all love each other, we all need each other. What else is there?"

Why did Hitchcock cut several of these lovebird shots? One can assume that he felt that they were "over the top" as symbolism. It is the kind of conceptual overlay that he usually resisted, believing that meaning develops naturally out of situation and character, as well as image. Yet he kept the association of Cathy with the lovebirds since she is the most innocent and therefore the most vulnerable character, and it was important to him that this innocence be accompanied by an "optimistic note," one that implies hope for the next generation.

Hunter's original ending, clearly designed to be the climax of the film, is the final bird attack upon the family as they flee in Mitch's sports car. During production the director deleted this last scene and substituted the one we see in the film, as the car slowly moves out towards the distant horizon, while the presently quiescent birds fill the entire space. Hitchcock even withheld the traditional "The End" title to preserve the open-endedness of the new conclusion. He told Hunter that one last bird attack would have been "superfluous," which did not satisfy the writer. Yet Hitchcock was convinced that he was right; he wrote to an exhibitor in England,

"I did have a further ending with a final attack on the automobile as it raced away, but I cut it out because it was so repetitious that the thing was anticlimactic."[23]

Hitchcock told Truffaut that he created a number of new shots while filming, a departure from his usual procedure, because he had discovered "weaknesses" in the screenplay. He mentioned specifically that in the scene following the finch attack from the chimney, he decided to shoot Lydia's horrified actions from Melanie's point of view to highlight her growing awareness of the deepening calamity, and that he inserted the broken teacups in the Fawcett-farm scene to add plausibility to Lydia's decision to search the house. During production he also created a scene that does not exist in the Hunter screenplay in which the unseen birds attack the Brenner house, one of the tensest, most frightening scenes in the film because the characters and the audience are forced to imagine the number and ferocity of the murderous attackers outside of the house as the threatening noise of the birds fills the soundtrack. Unlike the shots the director added to Stefano's script, these new shots in *The Birds* are thematic, as Hitchcock attempted to deepen character by expanding the subjective treatment of his material.

Hunter's reaction when he first saw the finished film at the Museum of Modern Art in 1963 was one of dismay, particularly regarding the new "non-ending." His surmise was that Hitchcock had decided to go for "high art" rather than suspense and action when he chose the alternative conclusion. He told us that the film should have been only about the bird attacks, not about the ambiguity of the human response to catastrophe, human relationships, or, as Hitchcock explained later to Truffaut, about the transformation of "a wealthy, shallow playgirl."[24]

Was Hunter accurate? Robert Kapsis certainly supports the writer in his book on Hitchcock. In his view, the glorification of the director on the part of Truffaut and his French New Wave colleagues had influenced Hitchcock to make an explicitly "arty" film that could simultaneously satisfy the audience who wanted more shock on the order of *Psycho*.[25] Hitchcock seems to have failed to communicate this goal to his screenwriter, who remained convinced that their main purpose should have been to "scare the hell out of people." In our interview Hunter said, "I think he was a little sad about *The Birds*. He was disappointed with it, and I was, too. He was disappointed with the audience's reaction at MOMA. I think I may have been even more disappointed because he was so sure he was entering 'the golden age' of his achievements. He put it in just those words. In many respects, what is underappreciated about *The Birds* is what he achieved without *Star Wars* technology. . . . Look at what he accomplished with hand puppets, animated and mechanical birds, mattes, and double exposure . . . and he had never done that at all. This was the most courageous film he ever made. He took a lot of risks. The sadness is he didn't have the courage to make it what it demanded to be. It didn't demand to be an art film. . . . They [the audience] should have come out of there screaming."[26]

Despite this lack of communication, we believe that *The Birds* is a major Hitchcock film because of these remarkable technical achievements, the stunning violence of the bird attacks, and—notwithstanding Hitchcock's and Hunter's conflicts and struggles with the character of Melanie—the complexities of the characters' personal relationships. And Hunter's work on the development of Melanie led directly to the deeper psychological nuances that he and his successor, Jay Presson Allen, brought to Marnie Edgar.

Marnie

Marnie was the result of one of the most complex collaborations in Hitchcock's career. Stefano, Hunter, and Allen all worked on this script at one time or another. The Winston Graham novel is both realistic and psychological and has more characters and scenes than the literary sources of *Psycho* or *The Birds*. This made the task of screenwriting more challenging because, in order to translate the book to the screen, episodes and characters from the novel needed to be eliminated, or at least combined or compressed. It is the only one of the three films that had a fully articulated treatment composed as a prelude to the composition of the screenplay, written by Joseph Stefano, which Hitchcock abridged before he passed it on to Evan Hunter in 1962, who was the first actual screenwriter. Working in concert with Hitchcock for three months in the spring of 1961, Stefano, as we have pointed out, expected to write the screenplay for Grace Kelly as the film's star. In a 161-page treatment titled "Alfred Hitchcock's *Marnie*," dated June 9, 1961, he transposed Winston Graham's 1961 English novel to an American setting, made Mark a more complex and darker character, and played up Marnie's sexual frigidity.

Following the novel's plot for the most part, much of what Stefano wrote went into Hunter's later screenplay and closely resembles parts of the film, particularly the opening on the train platform. But there are significant differences. Like the novel and Hunter's script, the character Terry Holbrook, Mark's partner and rival, appears here, as does Dr. Roman, the psychiatrist who treats Marnie at Mark's behest. The scene of Marnie working in and robbing a movie theater that reappears also in Hunter's work and Allen's script, but not the finished film, is here too, as is her second attempt to rob Rutland's after the fox hunt. Her mother's murder of the newborn child is preserved from the novel, as are the comforting characters Lucy Nye and Uncle Stephen. After her mother's death from a stroke, Marnie also has her moment of awareness about how her own view of love and sex was distorted by her mother, and she throws money from the robbery into her mother's grave in anger. At the conclusion, as in the book, Marnie is tricked into the hands of the police by Terry, but Dr. Roman and Mark are there for her, and Mark vows to wait for a woman who may have to go to jail but who now defines herself as "Mrs. Rutland."

Stefano retained the more visceral sense of social class and of the transgression of class boundaries that is a marked characteristic of the novel. He was especially pleased with the opportunity to depict the affluence and glamour that the street urchin rises to and her consciousness of class differences. As he told Tony Moral, the project was his opportunity to move up to "Park Avenue" in his work for the director, after the lower-class "depression world of *Psycho*,"[27] and markers for class are unmistakable in his text. In Stefano's treatment, when Mark "captures" Marnie at Garrod's after she has robbed the safe at Rutland's, she appeals to his sympathy as a poor orphan of the streets and links her "problem" to the squalor, abuse, and deprivation of her lower-class origins: "I always seem to have two drives at the same time. One belongs to me, the girl I'm trying to be, and the other to the little lost girl in Norfolk [Virginia], the child of the streets. I mean, I'm not hungry anymore, and I'm not teased and treated like dirt, but it's as if I still want to react as if I were. I can't explain it, Mark." Later, she harps on the "class" boundaries between them to explain why she needed to discourage Mark's attention: "I knew nothing could come of us. You're Main Line . . . and I'm . . . something sucked up in the vacuum cleaner." Later, as a ploy to gain his sympathy, she tells him that as a child she and her mother were on welfare.

Mark is both a more controlling and physical presence in Stefano's treatment than he is in the novel, and he wants to "cure" Marnie and dominate her. The sexual themes of the novel are exaggerated, particularly the discussion of frigidity, which is connected explicitly to Marnie's thievery, although it is not in the novel. As a result, the treatment becomes more of a psychological case history, focusing on her substituting theft for sex, while Mark's attraction to and "love" for Marnie is turned explicitly into a fetish, both of which motifs would be retained by Hunter and further developed by Allen. Even with these differences, Stefano stays close to the book's structure, preserving many of its most dramatic lines in key scenes.

As we have discussed earlier, Evan Hunter was the next writer assigned to the project, and he began his story conferences with Hitchcock while the director was still in production on *The Birds*. Yet this second collaboration ended prematurely because of a falling out precipitated by Hunter's reluctance to include what he considered to be a rape of Marnie by Mark, even though it is a key scene in the novel. Years later, Hunter told us that "when they were still shooting *The Birds* I went out to San Francisco to discuss *Marnie* with him, and I told him about my qualms about the scene, and he said, 'Don't worry about that.' It just seemed to me to go against every precept. I don't care who was playing it, even Cary Grant, it would still be a rapist. I just don't know how to make a rapist sympathetic." The passage of time did not soften Hunter's antipathy towards the scene; in 2001 he felt just as strongly about the stand he took as he did in 1963. (We joked with him that he was fired for being "prematurely politically correct.") He was also aware that Jay Presson Allen later remarked that the "rape" scene was the reason "why Hitchcock wanted to do the film," and she herself had no problem writing it. She said that Hunter's refusal to write the scene was essentially his "ticket back home." (The film critic Robin Wood asked Allen at a Hitchcock gathering in 1999 if she considered the forced sex between the frozen Marnie and the overpowering yet surprisingly tender Mark a "rape," since he himself did not. Allen agreed with Wood that the tenderness Mark shows for Marnie is always an inextricable part of his sexual desire, and thus the act on the honeymoon is not one of violence but of love. In fact, Allen's stage directions for the scene in her script emphasize that he takes her "with love.") Still, Hunter wondered if Hitchcock's own conflicted feelings for Tippi Hedren caused the director to overstep boundaries of craft and taste that he would not.[28]

Significantly, Hunter added a new psychological trauma from Marnie's childhood to account for her deep neurosis. This was a revelation at the end different than the one in the book and in the Stefano treatment, and one that would receive still another variation in Allen's final screenplays and the finished film. After consultation with a psychiatrist he knew,

Hunter made the traumatic event that has caused most of her neurotic symptoms Marnie's having witnessed as a child her mother's murder of a drunken sailor, a memory Marnie had repressed. The psychologist endorsed Hunter's version as more "valid" than the one in the novel, and the writer and Hitchcock continued to consult several psychiatrists and make inquiries about case histories to strengthen the psychological dimension of the film and Marnie's scenes with Dr. Roman. At Hitchcock's direction, Hunter wrote a letter to Tippi Hedren explaining in oedipal terms the impact of the trauma he had created on Marnie's later thievery and her feelings toward Mark's sexual advances. Hunter related the killing of the sailor to deep-seated neuroses stemming from Marnie's unresolved feelings about the death at sea of her father (a background presence from the novel that he had retained), which took place at essentially the same time as the murder.[29] Looking at this letter and the extent of Hunter's and Hitchcock's involvement in and commitment to psychological explanations of the main character's behavior, it is possible to see the genesis of the overly explicit psychologizing in the dialogue of the finished film.

When Jay Presson Allen was hired to work on the project in June 1963, she was given a scene synopsis by Hitchcock that came directly from Hunter's script, though she was never told that it came from a previous writer—as was also the case when Hunter was given a treatment for *Marnie* that he did not know was based on one by Joseph Stefano. Actual scenes from Hunter's script and verbatim dialogue appear in Allen's screenplay. The biggest change that Allen introduced into the story was the expansion of the Mark Rutland role, which accommodated the star power of Sean Connery and the introduction of a new woman character, Lil, to create romantic conflict. She also dropped the psychiatrist character and the character of Terry, both of whom came from the novel and were retained by Stefano and Hunter, and replaced Mark's mother with his father. This development shifted the psychological dynamic of the finished film when compared to the Stefano treatment and the Hunter drafts, both of which stayed much closer to the characterization in Winston Graham's novel.

The synopsis Allen was given also ended with Marnie going to prison, knowing that Mark will wait for her, which is not made explicit even in the novel. Interestingly, her mother, not Marnie, had killed the sailor in this version, as in Hunter's screenplay. Thus the ending of Allen's script differs significantly from the previous ones and gives Mark more control over Marnie's fate.

The main difference between Allen's first and second drafts is that the extensive dialogue in her first draft has been cut significantly. Allen was a playwright after all, and this was her first screenplay, so the director was busier than usual in asking for less talk and more opportunities for visual storytelling. In addition to precisely delineated upper-class credentials for the Rutlands, Mark's jaguarundi speech was one of Allen's original contributions, as was all the animal imagery that permeates the verbal content of the finished film. Allen remarked to us that the animal/hunting motif was hers, but that Hitchcock strongly endorsed it. Mark's speech, one of the best in the film, was gradually shortened through Allen's various drafts. In this second draft it still contains the following interesting lines: "Jaguarundis can't be bent or broken. If you menace them, they become even more dangerous. If they're mishandled . . . well, like many wild things, their final sanctuary is voluntary death." Since Marnie attempts suicide later in the film, it is somewhat surprising that Hitchcock edited this dialogue, though perhaps he didn't want the audience to expect Marnie's unsuccessful try at drowning herself.

The third draft included some revelatory changes. For the first time, the expressionistic red flashes appear in the script when Marnie is overcome by fear (though at this point they still do not appear in the concluding flashback scene). In our conversation, Allen mentioned that the red suffusions were Hitchcock's idea and that she incorporated them into the script after one of their working sessions, so clearly these talks continued as she worked on the various drafts. The "Call for the Doctor" song sung by the children outside Mrs. Edgar's Baltimore home is included in this third draft. And in the script's final sequence, a boy cleans off streaks of rain from the windshield of Mark's car as he drives away with Marnie. Presumably at Hitchcock's request, Allen was working to introduce both visual and verbal cues to Marnie's sickness and the beginning of her movement toward health.

Curiously, two scenes from the novel, Stefano's treatment, and Hunter's script remain in this third draft that would not be cut until the final shooting script. One is a flashback to the young Marnie fighting with a group of girls who have attacked her after she has stolen some perfume from a shop. The other is a scene that was actually written by Evan Hunter but which is included in every draft by Hunter and Allen until the last, even though Allen obviously knew it wasn't hers. It takes place in a projectionist's booth in a movie theater; we discover through the dialogue that

Marnie, a cashier at the theater, has stolen the evening's take from the cash box. This scene is roughly based on a corresponding one in the novel that is told from Marnie's first-person point of view. Presumably Hitchcock at first thought the scene was necessary to show Marnie's development as a compulsive thief but finally cut it because it is a "non-scene" scene, or because it presents Marnie in a more plebian working setting than he wanted the character to have. He would rely on Marnie's serial robberies of office safes to make the same point, though the only one included in the diegesis before her robbery of Rutland's is that of Strutt, though here we see only the robbery victim and the empty safe.

In the final draft, dated September 24, 1963, the flashback to Marnie's childhood fight remains, though it has been marked as follows: "Consult Jay about this scene." The jaguarundi speech is marked "literary??," which gives us Hitchcock's possible motivation for cutting it. The window-wiper closing is gone, but the projectionist scene is still here. And this draft is a shooting script—presumably Hitchcock did the shot breakdown himself, since Allen was a novice screenwriter. As in the case of *Psycho,* this meant indications in the script for the most important camera angles and placements—with many decisions for the less dramatic effects to be made during the shooting. Still another draft exists, one also marked "shooting script" and dated October 9, 1963. There are still some X's through lines of dialogue, and some new bits of dialogue have been added in longhand by the director. The fight is here, and, of course, so is the projectionist scene. Were these scenes shot and cut during postproduction? No evidence exists that will answer this question definitively. Though it would have been unusual, there is some precedent in Hitchcock's work for dropping scenes entirely that had been shot (for example, the "birds of the world unite" scene in *The Birds).*

The last work that Jay Presson Allen did on the film was sent by her to Hitchcock on December 16 from Cairo. It is a rewritten version of the scene in which Marnie goes home for the first time in the movie to visit her mother. It is accompanied by the following note:

> Dear Hitch—
> Sorry to be so slow with this scene, but here it finally is—IN TIME, I hope. Who is Bernice [the director had changed the name Allen had given Marnie's mother]? What is she? As for ME—I am long ago and FAR away.
> Much love, Jay.[30]

Though Allen is clearly distancing herself from the project and turning it completely over to the director, she also is reaffirming her support for the script and the excellent rapport that marked their collaboration.

A comparison of Allen's shooting script to the finished film reveals that, as in the case of the other two projects, the detailed shot breakdown in the script served only as a rough blueprint for the finished film, which contains many more shots and many more cuts than are indicated in the script. For example, the second scene of the film, which takes place entirely in Strutt's office after he discovers the robbery, is broken down in the script into fifteen shots, each characterized by camera distance (i.e., MED SHOT); camera movement, if there is any; camera perspective, if it is a POV shot; and by the number of characters in the shot. The scene on film, however, consists of twenty-one shots, and many differ from the shot descriptions in the script. As the scene develops in the script, Strutt and the detectives are usually in the shot together, with an occasional close shot of Strutt. In the film, they are never in the shot together until Strutt crosses the room to greet Mark Rutland. Clearly, as Hitchcock addressed the camera setups for this scene, he decided to isolate Strutt in close shots, emphasizing the emotional distance between him and the slightly condescending detectives. As in the case of *Psycho* and *The Birds,* this increase in the number of shots and cuts in the finished film when compared to the shooting script is characteristic of most of the scenes and reveals that, despite his frequent protestations in interviews, Hitchcock did do some genuine creative work with his cinematographer and editor after production began.

As far as the director and screenwriter were concerned, though, the writer's work was completed when a revised script was marked "Final": for example, Joseph Stefano proudly signed copies of the November 10, 1959, script of *Psycho,* indicating that he considered this version the best representation of his work on the project. And though the plot and characters were developed in collaboration with Hitchcock as they adapted the novel, and camera placements in this script are largely Hitchcock's, the dialogue and stage directions were his and his alone. In this sense, Stefano "wrote the script" for this immensely important and influential film.

However, the writers also all agree that Hitchcock gave them little public credit for their work after a film had succeeded, and certainly if it did not. Often this lack of recognition resulted from simple omission— the director simply did not mention them in interviews. For example, he never mentioned Joseph Stefano's name to Francois Truffaut when they discussed *Psycho.* He didn't mention Evan Hunter's name, either, though he does imply a criticism of his writer's script when he says in the interview that "something happened to me that was altogether new in my experience: I began to study the scenario as we went along, and I saw that there were weaknesses in it. This emotional siege I went through served to bring out an additional creative sense in me."[31] And he proceeds to explain the various shots that he improvised on the set that had not been in the script, storyboarded, or even in his own mind when production began, contrary to his traditional working methods and induced by what he felt was an insufficiency of Hunter's script. As for *Marnie,* again the author Jay Presson Allen's name is never mentioned in the interview.

Why such lack of recognition from Hitchcock? Some of it was certainly due to ego. But such an answer is too simplistic to account fully for his disregard for his writers' work after they had been employed by him. Actors often indicated that he gave them no signs of approval about their performances and little recognition in general. (Even Hilton Green, who was assistant director on *Psycho* and unit manager on *Marnie* and remains one of the staunchest defenders of Hitchcock's warmth and humanity, admitted that when he joined Hitchcock's television crew in the 1950s, the director's lack of a response to him after several days of work convinced him he was about to be fired.) Our conclusion is that Hitchcock regarded his writers as he did his other collaborators—his assistant director, his production designer, and his editor: as absolutely essential professionals whose job was to ensure that his particular style of filmmaking was fully realized on the screen. He seemed to feel that no approval was necessary for people simply doing their jobs, or even doing their jobs very well, despite the fact that he hungered for recognition himself and felt slighted by Hollywood throughout his life. But when it came to his collaborators or crew, he felt that they worked for *him* and, ultimately, that it was *his* film. His was the creative mind that utilized and synthesized all the other contributors' efforts, and he was extremely possessive of the finished product and resisted sharing credit. Though film criticism and theory might challenge his assumptions, for Hitchcock the director *was* the author, and he wanted the critics and the public to consider the films he directed as *his* films. Although at times in his career he had to battle producers like Selznick to fulfill that role, it was the only one that could encompass his personal definition of filmmaking.

CHAPTER 4

Final Drafts

The Shooting Scripts

An analysis of the shooting scripts as texts is a valid, even necessary process for Hitchcock studies on several accounts. These scripts represent the fullest extent of the collaborative process that began when the writer first sat with the director in his office to discuss the possibilities for narrative and character development inherent in the source material; they also highlight the particular verbal talents of the writers, talents that Hitchcock himself did not possess; and they demonstrate how the characters existed in Hitchcock's mind before the actors began to mold them to their own styles and personalities. So in a book in which we are primarily interested in Hitchcock's work with his writers, it is important to examine the characters and themes of the shooting scripts rather than of the films themselves, which has been done quite exhaustively by many critics and theorists.

Psycho

Stefano begins his *Psycho* screenplay with directions that indicate a helicopter shot over Phoenix in which the social and psychological scenery becomes increasingly shabby and sinister as the camera approaches the hotel where Marion and Sam have just finished their mid-afternoon assignation: "The very geography seems to give us a climate of nefariousness, of back-doorness, dark and shadowy. And secret. . . . We pause long enough to establish the shoddy character of this hotel. Its open, curtainless windows, its silent resigned look so characteristic of such hole-and-corner hotels." As in a novel or play, Stefano uses setting to define character and conflict, both of which are revealed in the opening scene to follow.

In creating the postcoital hotel-room scene as the opening sequence of the November 10 screenplay of *Psycho,* Joseph Stefano introduces us to Marion Crane, whose goal—the desire to make this relationship with her lover permanent—becomes the central focus of the narrative for the first quarter of the script. Stefano skillfully uses the mise-en-scène of the hotel room, as described by the stage directions, to reinforce Marion's cramped, restricted life, while he created dialogue for her that makes her humanity compelling. Inside the room, the camera reveals "[a] small room, a slow fan buzzing on a shelf above the narrow bed." Marion, the directions continue, has a face that "seen in the dimness of the room, betrays a certain inner-tension, worrisome conflicts." And increasing the growing tone of desperation, he adds, "She is . . . an attractive girl nearing the end of her twenties and her rope."

The dialogue now establishes Marion's character as she interacts with Sam. She is a compassionate person who has sacrificed much in her life, and her sincerity and vulnerability seem at variance with the surroundings. Her impatient, somewhat long-suffering matter-of-factness contrasts with Sam's superficial good cheer. The dialogue tells us right away that Sam Loomis, who is described as "a good-looking sensual man" with "humorous eyes," is unable to give Marion the respectability and emotional security she craves. Her reply to his suggestion that they linger a while longer in the room is intended to make this painfully evident: "Checking out time is three P.M.," she says. "Hotels of this sort aren't interested in you when you come in, but when your time's up . . . (a small anguish) Sam, I hate having to be with you in a place like this." When Sam goes to the window, partially to avoid and deflect what she is saying, Stefano's directions indicate that it is the hotel setting that embodies repugnance: "[T]he hot sun glares into the room, revealing it in all its shabbiness and sordidness as if corroborating Mary's words and attitude." The dialogue then reinforces and extends these directions and reveals more about the lives of these two and the deprivation and frustration they are living with.

In response to Sam's anger at "sweating" to "pay off" his father's debts and ex-wife's alimony, Marion is charitable and self-sacrificing when she says, "I pay, too. They also pay who meet in hotel rooms," a line that echoes the fatalistic conclusion of Milton's sonnet "On His Blindness": "They also serve who only stand and wait." And when Sam descends into bitterness about the deprivation that she would have to endure if they married ("When I send my ex-wife her money, you can lick the stamps"), Stefano makes her self-denial poignant: "I'll lick the stamps," she answers.

Like the dismal hotel room, which is all they can afford, Stefano situates Marion and Sam on the margins of 1950s consumer culture, as neither can substantially participate in the material comforts of the postwar economic expansion that by 1960 had dramatically broadened the American middle class. This is further evident in Marion's Phoenix workplace, which lacks the basic comfort of air conditioning; in her dark, spare, colorless bedroom; in her instantly disposable used car; and in Sam's living quarters at the back of the hardware store in Fairvale, where he works to pay off his father's debts. Both attribute the inertia in their relationship to a lack of money, a deficiency that motivates the sympathetic Marion's desperate act. As David Thomson has remarked in relation to other Hollywood films of the period, "we need to stress one remarkable thing: an American film has begun (in the famously developing city of Phoenix—a miracle of new urban life) in which the hopes and desires of two mature people are overshadowed by lack of money and social freedom."[1]

In addition to the dialogue and directions, the writer further establishes a sympathetic Marion by contrasting her with the film's minor characters, whom she encounters after the hotel-room scene: the cautious Lowery; the voluble but tranquilized Caroline; the officious and menacing highway patrolman; the unctuous used-car salesman, California Charley; and in particular the "pitifully" vulgar Cassidy. When we hear Cassidy's voice exclaim, "Well, I ain't about to kiss off forty thousand dollars! I'll get it back, and if any of it is missin' I'll replace it with her fine soft flesh! I'll track her, never you doubt it!", these lines not only reemphasize Cassidy's cruelty and crudity toward her but also explicitly link sex and violence.

At this point, Stefano introduces the almost equally compelling character of Norman into the screenplay. As Marion climbs the porch at the Bates Motel where he is waiting for her in the rain, Stefano's directions indicate a young man who is in his "late twenties, thin and tall," and "soft-spoken and hesitant." In fact, the writer's depiction of Norman was facilitated by his knowledge that Anthony Perkins was to play the role and his subsequent meetings with the actor. He adds that there "is something almost sadly touching in his manner, in his look," an aspect of Norman that he elaborates in the following moment. Norman's gentle manner makes Marion's nervousness and anxiety disappear, and her friendliness toward him is contagious: "[Her] impatience goes and she smiles and this makes [Norman] almost smile." Responding to her warmth, he tells her in lines that respond directly to her femininity, "You have something most girls never have. . . . There's no name for it. . . . But it's something that, that puts a person at ease." Clearly this moment in the script was intended to establish their kindness and congeniality, to suggest their rapport and kinship, as well as Norman's unease around women.

The physical surroundings of the motel and house and the dialogue also signify that Norman lives even more on the margins of the culture, both personally and economically, than Marion and Sam do. To use the sheriff's later words, he "lives like a hermit," running a motel that attracts a trickle of customers each month because the highway has been moved. The sparseness of his existence—emblematized in his antiquated possessions and his thrifty and austere habits—has fed his isolation, which in turn has alienated him from his fellow human beings and from the postwar consumer culture that as a motel owner he is supposed to be an integral part of. On a material level, his life is even starker than Marion's and Sam's "working-class" existence.

Stefano, of course, was faced with the challenge of how to make "Mother," whom we first encounter as a shadow and a voice, a real, almost physical presence in the film so that first-time viewers would accept her as an actual character. As a result, the initial encounter between Norman and Mother in the script is punctuated by the shrill, angry voice that emanates from the decaying house on the hill above the motel, a voice that, with the image of an old woman's shadow in the upstairs window, can easily convince an audience that Norman's invalid mother is truly in her room, constantly condemning her weak-willed son. Mother also becomes a central presence in the dialogue for the rest of this sequence and the entire screenplay, during which her unseen presence will make her the moving force in the narrative.

Stefano defines both characters more clearly through their reaction and responses to the other. Norman in this scene is not simply self-revealing and self-loathing, especially in relation to Mother, but gently ironic and psychologically astute. This Norman understands and identifies with what he learns of Marion's situation even before she identifies with him. They begin their "supper" in the motel parlor with a discussion of his hobby: taxidermy, stuffing birds. Stefano and Hitchcock added the backdrop of the frightening stuffed birds to the mise-en-scène to suggest something ominous, just as the setting of the hotel room was used earlier to suggest sordidness. The pathos of Norman's existence and his vulnerability where women are concerned are intensified here through Marion's reactions. The writer's directions indicate that Marion "looks at him with some compassion" as he discusses his circumscribed existence: she is not yet frightened by his words or manner. The antithesis of Cassidy and his disparaging of Marion's existence, Norman speculates that she has "never had an empty moment in [her] whole life," a statement that she disputes. Then the writer has him ask her two questions that are eerily perceptive and confronting and that precipitate perhaps the best dialogue in the film: "Where are you going?" he asks, and, "What are you running away from?" Marion answers the first with a "wistful smile" and a moment of self-realization: "I'm looking for a private island," she replies, Stefano's metaphor for her desperate attempt to escape her situation that also appears in the first scene but was dropped from the film. Without letting her answer the second question, Norman responds with some of the most powerful lines in all of Hitchcock: "People never run away from anything. You know what I think? We're all in our private traps, clamped in them, and none of us can ever climb out. We scratch and claw, but only at the air, only at each other, and for all of it we never budge an inch." The psychologically loaded vision of human inertia and immobility conveyed here, which denies the possibility of change and growth, is in retrospect an apt metaphor for Norman's own psychosis and his bond with Mother, but clearly Stefano also intends it to connect to the stasis of Mary's life and the desperation of her theft. It inspires in her a moment of self-recognition and revelation as she responds, "Sometimes we deliberately step into those traps."

Norman's subsequent detailing of the "trap" he was born into—including his account of his father's death, his mother's lover and his death, and her ensuing "illness"—indicates the depth of his "commitment" to Mother, whom he cannot think of abandoning: "When you love someone, you don't do that to them, even if you hate them," he says. "Oh, I don't hate *her*. I hate . . . what she's become. I hate the illness," the repetition of this word underscoring his sensitivity, perception, and compassion. However, Norman's clarification is followed by a confrontation with Marion over her suggestion that he "put [Mother] in . . . someplace." Here Norman's character appears to turn, momentarily reflecting the predatory birds in the background. According to the script, after Marion speaks, "She hesitates [and] Norman turns slowly, looking at her with a striking coldness." As he rebukes her for suggesting that Mother be confined in a "madhouse" and accuses her of being uncaring, the directions further indicate that Norman speaks to her with a "coldness" that turns to "tight fury" and then to "high fury," as he ridicules her excuse that she meant well: "Well? You meant well? People always mean well, they cluck their thick tongues and shake their heads and suggest so very delicately that. . . ." But as angry as Norman becomes, and as much as Marion is unnerved and frightened by his outburst, the directions indicate that his emotions soon calm, and she, in response, is overcome with compassion for him: "The fury suddenly dies, abruptly and completely, and he sinks back into his chair. There is a brief silence. [Marion] watches the troubled man, [and] is almost physically pained by his anguish."

It is at this point that Stefano uses a variation of the line about madness in Bloch, but he elevates it and its context by having Norman first tacitly agree with Marion about institutionalizing Mother: "I've suggested it myself. But I hate to think such a thing. . . . [I]t's just that sometimes she goes a little mad. *We all go a little mad sometimes. Haven't you?*" (italics added). In the script, Norman speaks the final line after a reflective pause, not in the heat of anger, with introspection and understanding instead of rage, and unlike his dialogue in the book, his final two words connect this idea of madness directly to Marion, just as he connects Marion to Mother and himself.

Madness enters explicitly in the subsequent shower murder sequence, which Stefano depicts in substantial detail in five distinct scenes that essentially summarize what appears on the screen and anticipate the celebrated storyboards. While this sequence lacks the precise shot-by-shot of the film and occupies slightly more than a page of the script, the visual specificity indicates how thoroughly Stefano had been involved with the director in planning and conceptualizing what eventually appeared on the screen. In a general sense, the descriptions not only of Marion's gestures and movements but also of her reactions and emotions are clearly stage directions, as can be seen when she enters the shower:

INT. MARY IN SHOWER

Over the bar on which hangs the shower curtain, we can see the bathroom door, not entirely closed. For a moment we watch Mary as she washes and soaps herself. **There is still a small worry in her eyes, but generally she looks somewhat relieved.**

Now we see the bathroom door being pushed slowly open. The noise of the shower drowns out any sound. The door is then slowly and carefully closed. And we see the shadow of a woman fall across the shower curtain. Mary's back is turned to the curtain. The white

brightness of the bathroom is almost blinding. Suddenly we see the
hand reach up, grasp the shower curtain, rip it aside. (Emphasis added)

While his indication that she "generally looks somewhat relieved" does not account for the extent of cleansing and renewal that Marion conveys in the film as she begins her shower, Stefano emphasizes her reactions to the "knife slashing": her "look of pure horror," her "terrible groan" and "gulps of screaming," and then the "dreadful thump" of her falling body. He describes the madwoman who has committed the murder as she leaves the bathroom ("face contorted," her "head wild with hair"), and then the positioning of Marion's body at the base of the shower both in terms of camera movement and what the audience will see.

Following this scene, even more visual detail is employed in the screenplay to describe Norman's elaborate cleanup, including his movements, gestures, timing, and reactions. Five pages of Stefano's November 10 screenplay are devoted to it and to the disposal of Marion's car, and the whole sequence is divided into seventeen numbered scenes. There are even indications of specific camera angles and camera movement, showing that Hitchcock and Stefano planned this together very thoroughly. Since there could be no dialogue at this point in the film, Stefano wrote directions that emphasize Norman's point of view and reactions—to connect him to what the audience would experience at this point—and he and Hitchcock added the car's moment of hesitation before sinking to increase suspense. With the exception of notations in the screenplay, such as an airplane that flies overhead with a prominently heard motor, the script is a virtual description of what we see on screen. Stefano's directions specify that Norman's anxiety grows as the car hesitates before sinking into the swamp, and they include both visual and auditory detail:

He looks at the car. More than two-thirds of it have already sunk into
the swamp. The trunk alone seems to hold poised above the sand and
*slime, as if refusing to go the rest of the way. **Norman begins to panic.***
. . . [But] slowly the car sinks, until finally it is gone and we hear only
the gentle plop of the swamp's final gulp, and see only the small after
bubble, like a visual burp. (Emphasis added)

In essence, this sequence is a self-contained unit of action with a new protagonist who has replaced Marion, a new conflict, and a new resolution.

While we are still trying to assimilate the sudden, horrifying loss of the protagonist of the first forty-five minutes of the film, we are subliminally encouraged to sympathize with Norman as he desperately tries to cover up the murder Mother in her insanity has just committed.

At this point in the screenplay, a third plot is introduced with the arrival of Lila at Sam's hardware store. The new protagonist is the combined team of Sam/Lila, and their goal is to determine what has become of the missing Mary. Norman becomes the antagonist—albeit still a partially sympathetic one, since we believe his lies to Sam and Arbogast are used to cover up something his monstrous mother has done, not Norman himself.

The search for Marion culminates when Sam/Lila confront Norman at the Bates Motel and Lila is able to slip away to investigate the house. The novel has two distinct chapters at this point—the first with Norman and Sam talking and drinking as Lila goes off, the second with her searching the house—but to build suspense the screenplay combines the two actions. As in the earlier scene of Marion undressing in her room with Norman spying through a peephole, this scene is another example of the crucial difference between what a novel is limited to and the narrative possibilities of film.

The encounter is marked by an assertive and aggressive Sam confronting Norman and insisting that Norman wants to escape his isolation at the motel and relocate to a new town where he can more easily "hide" Mother. Stefano developed this scene as a dramatic contrast to the earlier one between Marion and Norman: what his antagonist needs, Sam claims, is money—namely, forty thousand dollars. He begins by noting Norman's isolation and loneliness, how it would drive him "crazy." "I'd do just about anything to get away," Sam exclaims. "Wouldn't you? . . . I think if you saw a chance to get out from under . . . you'd unload this place. . . ." Provoked by this challenge, Norman becomes angrily defensive, and the compelling character of the parlor scene turns angry and desperate: "This place! This isn't 'a place.' It's my only world. I grew up in that house back there. I was a happy child. My mother and I . . . we were more than happy!" This last line gives Sam the opportunity to bait Norman, just as Arbogast had earlier, and to get crucial information about Mother:

SAM: And now that your mother's dead?
Norman snaps a sharp, fast, ugly look at him.
NORMAN: My mother is not dead!
SAM: *(Softly)* I didn't think so.

At the same time that Sam extracts this admission from Norman, Lila investigates the house, beginning with "Mother's room." The screenplay's directions indicate the depth of her distress at what she observes, her curiosity mixed with an even more intense repulsion:

LILA'S VOICE: Mrs. Bates?
There is quiet for a moment, then the door begins to open slowly, and we see Lila. She stands on the threshold, looking in at the room, **instantly disturbed by it, almost chilled, her expression indicating an impulse to close the door and go away from this room forever.** *After a moment, she enters, leaving the door open behind her. CAMERA PULLS BACK AND AWAY and we now see the room as LILA sees it.* (Emphasis added)

The directions continue this tone as she moves on to Norman's infantilized bedroom:

Lila is standing in the doorway, staring at the room in **sick dismay. The room is grotesque, a horrible, ludicrous fantasy of childhood held beyond the point of decency.** (Emphasis added)

And after opening a "plain-bound book," which is clearly pornographic:

Her eyes go wide in shock. And then there is disgust. *She slams the book closed, drops it.* (Emphasis added)

The next shot, marked INT. THE MOTEL OFFICE, has directions specifying that Norman displays the "stark, high sheen of a cornered animal" as Sam's interrogation intensifies, especially in relation to Mother:

SAM: *(Pressing)* You look frightened. Have I been saying something frightening?
NORMAN: I don't know what you've been saying.
SAM: I've been talking about your mother . . . about your motel. How are you going to do it?
NORMAN: Do what?
SAM: Buy a new one! In a new town! Where you won't have to hide

your mother! Where will you get the money to do that, Bates? . . .
Or do you already have it . . . socked away . . . a lot of it . . .
NORMAN: Leave me alone!
SAM: . . . Forty thousand dollars!
NORMAN: Leave me alone!
He is close to panic now. He turns, swiftly, dashes back into his private parlor. Sam goes quickly around the counter, follows.

As Norman's panic increases, Stefano's directions specify that he tries to escape from the motel parlor where they are talking, but he cannot. Sensing that Norman is about to divulge something momentous, and still believing that whatever he has done with Marion is about the stolen money (the film's MacGuffin), Sam hones in on him, using Mother as his lever, and the directions accentuate the specific visual terror of the moment:

SAM: I bet your mother knows where the money is. And what you
did to get it. And I think she'll tell us.
Something self-assured and confident in Sam's tone gives Norman a new, more terrified alarm. He turns his head, glances out the window at the old house. He looks back at Sam, and there is terror in his voice.

The potential discovery of "Mother" is what is terrifying Norman at this point in the screenplay. The very next shot, marked INT. UPSTAIRS HALL OF THE OLD HOUSE—DAY, returns the audience to Lila and describes her reaction as she exits Norman's room: "Lila, shaken and disturbed, almost sickened, is coming out of Norman's room."

What is most significant about the crosscutting of these two actions in the screenplay is the ways each character is revealed and the narrative is advanced. A new side of Sam is presented in the dialogue, just as a more troubling and pathological dimension of Norman is revealed and underscored in Lila's reactions to what she sees in his room. Sam's increasing assertiveness and confidence are matched by Norman's growing insecurity, panic, and violence. Simultaneously, as the directions indicate, Lila's discovery of Norman's history and of the world he and Mother inhabit is highlighted by her reactions of emotional and physical disgust, which foreshadow what the audience's own responses will soon be. Further linking these elements of character and narrative in the dialogue is the discussion of Mother that Sam initiates, a mother whom, he asserts, Norman must hide away for fear of the consequences her discovery would produce, and a mother who will be revealed shortly. Beginning in the fruit cellar, continuing through the psychiatrist's explanation, and concluding with Norman in the jail totally transformed into Mother in the final reverie in which he refuses to swat a fly, the final sequences of the screenplay completely combine the characters of Norman and Mother—his identity is conflated into hers, with all the positive qualities the audience has seen in him earlier now dissolved into pathology, as in the final image of the car being lifted from the swamp.

The Birds

Characterization and narrative development in the screenplay of *The Birds* are not as effectively integrated as they are in the screenplay of *Psycho,* but they still make for a classic film. Hunter and the director agreed that a human drama involving the interaction of characters the audience would identify with had to be integrated into the story of the attacks. But, as noted earlier, the two had conceptual differences, and during production Hitchcock second-guessed the screenplay that Hunter produced at many turns. Some of it he had rewritten; some of it he ignored; and some of the finished film he created himself, or improvised, on the set.[2]

Hunter set out to write a screwball comedy that turns darkly serious when the bird attacks begin.[3] He had in mind the great black-and-white screwball comedies of the 1930s, but he acknowledged that at the time "antic" comedy was not his strength as a writer. Years later, he asserted that "screwball comedy demands a very special kind of writing that derives more from situation than it does from character,"[4] something he had not really understood at the time.

Hunter's opening scene certainly has affinities to classic screwball comedy. There is the ostensible issue of mistaken identity in the pet shop; another common element of the screwball genre, social-class distinctions between the couple, are present in so far as Melanie appears to be an heiress and Mitch of the middle class; and the lovebirds, which are analogous to the intrusive animals occasionally found in such comedies, provide for a potentially farcical situation with sexual overtones. But Hunter's approach to these elements makes the encounter of Mitch and Melanie more akin to the first meetings between potential lovers in romantic, rather than screwball, comedies: lovers who begin with antagonism that masks a deeper level of attraction that the audience immediately picks up on.

Melanie is briefly described in the directions as a "young woman in her mid-twenties, sleekly groomed, exquisitely dressed with the sureness of a city dweller." Mitch is simply characterized as a "young man of twenty-nine or thirty" who is "handsome" and "well-dressed." When Mitch first recognizes Melanie and decides to play a joke on her by treating her like a salesgirl, she is in the pet shop trying to buy a myna bird, to teach it words that would shock a prim seventy-year-old aunt. Instead of the mad-cap flightiness of the screwball heroine, the narrative features Melanie's propensity for practical jokes. She has a "sureness," "purposefulness," and a "mischievous grin on her face," Hunter's directions specify, and she quickly decides to turn this inadvertent meeting with an attractive man into a prank:

> MITCH: I wonder if you could help me.
> MELANIE: What?
> MITCH: *(Deliberately and with a touch of hauteur)* I said I wonder if you could help me.
> CLOSE SHOT—MELANIE
> *A trifle annoyed by his manner at first. She is about to inform him, if you please, that she is not a shop girl. But then something rebellious flashes in her eyes and an idea comes to her.*
> MELANIE: *(solicitously)* Yes, what was it you were looking for?
> MITCH: *(Deadpan)* Lovebirds.

We don't know at this moment that Mitch is playing with her and is one step ahead of her; we only wonder how long Melanie can maintain her pose as a shop girl.

Unlike a screwball scene, in which either the man or the woman has trouble understanding the other's motivation and/or goal and appears to be operating on a different plane of reality, here both characters settle quickly on the same double entendre for a flirtatious exchange, much like Tracy/Hepburn or Grant/Russell in a romantic comedy:

> MITCH: These are for my sister . . . her birthday, you see. As she'll be eleven and . . . well, frankly, I wouldn't want a pair of birds that were too demonstrative.

MELANIE: I understand completely, sir.

MITCH: At the same time, I wouldn't want birds that were aloof, either.

MELANIE: No, of course not.

MITCH: Do you have a pair that are just friendly?

In other words, the scene is amusing rather than "zany," and from that perspective the script is reminiscent of the first encounter of Lisa and Jefferies in *Rear Window*.

The fact that Mitch is aware of Melanie's true identity also separates the scene from an authentic screwball encounter. The males of classic screwball, such as the characters played by Cary Grant in *The Awful Truth* and *Bringing Up Baby,* are controlled by Irene Dunne's or Katherine Hepburn's unpredictable, spontaneous personality and behavior. Here Mitch not only is not fooled by Melanie's practical joke, but he also is able to turn the joke back on her. And his judgmental attitude toward Melanie regarding her current impersonation and her past "gilded-cage" episodes is certainly not typical of the tone of screwball.

As the narrative proceeds to Bodega Bay several scenes later, Hunter's directions indicate a close shot of the lovebirds bending in unison and straightening up as Melanie's sports car speeds around turns, continuing the comic tone of the opening scene. But the lovebirds play a more serious role from this point on, as the film begins to alter its comic tone and the emotional direction of the narrative. There is some comedy in the clerks in the rural post office/general store and their confusion over Cathy Brenner's name, but the screenplay moves in a more serious direction in Melanie's first encounter with Annie Hayworth, the schoolteacher. The romantic comedy starts to change shape into a domestic melodrama centered upon the issues of loneliness and isolation[5]: this melodrama will govern the interaction of the characters as the bird attacks begin, attacks that create still another kind of melodrama based on terror and suspense.

The domestic melodrama emerges immediately in Hunter's dialogue and directions in the first scene between Melanie and Annie, in which the unguarded schoolteacher quickly sizes up the socialite's interest in Mitch when Melanie stops at her house for information. There is no witty rivalry in their encounter as we would find in a screwball comedy, in which two women, often from different social classes, like these two, compete for the same man; instead, the screenplay moves toward melodrama even before there is any bird violence. In response to Melanie, Annie refers to herself as "an open book . . . or maybe a closed one," suggesting that she is hopelessly carrying a torch for Mitch, and Hunter's directions elaborate this by specifying that there is a "look of sad resignation on [Annie's] face," a directive intended to prepare the audience for more such emotional revelations and interactions rather than more comedy. So, as hints of comedy diminish, the script becomes closer to the "woman's picture" melodrama typical of Hollywood in the 1940s.

When Melanie is first attacked by the gull after she has surreptitiously delivered the lovebirds to the Brenner home, Hunter intensifies the domestic melodrama. It dominates the first Tides Restaurant scene when Mitch tends Melanie's wounds, especially in the encounter between Melanie and Lydia in which Hunter creates more tension and competition than in the earlier meeting between Melanie and Annie. After a mild bit of residual comic banter—Melanie tells him, "I *loathe* you. You have no manners. And you're arrogant and conceited"—Lydia appears. Hunter describes her as an "attractive" woman in her "late forties" (which seems a stretch if Mitch is supposed to be around thirty), and, like Melanie, Lydia seems to embody the city within her: "She speaks with the lively tempo of a city dweller." During her introduction to Melanie, Hunter's directions indicate that Lydia raises her eyebrows "ever so slightly" and that she sizes up the young woman disapprovingly as "one of Mitch's San Francisco chippies." When Mitch invites Melanie to dinner, Lydia acts surprised and hesitant, since she suspects that this young woman has designs on Mitch. Then, when she learns that Melanie has brought "lovebirds" for Cathy's birthday, the dialogue and directions make her concern abundantly clear:

LYDIA: *(Understanding completely now)* Love birds, I see.

While hardly direct hostility, Lydia's response indicates resistance, if not antagonism, to this potential rival for her son's affection. Unlike the earlier interaction between Mitch and Melanie, there is no comedy here, just as there was none between Melanie and Annie; instead there are the seeds of a melodrama based on the competition between a mother and a potential lover.

This tension continues during dinner, preceded by some lingering comic dialogue that contrasts human appetites with the Brenners' chickens refusing to eat, and later when Cathy pokes fun at Mitch's profession as a criminal lawyer, especially at the hoods and the wife murderer he has represented. But Hunter brings the mother/lover plot to the fore again. When Lydia is alone with her son in the kitchen, she praises Melanie's charm and looks and attempts to assess the degree of her son's attachment to this new woman with a question about how long Mitch has known her. When Mitch replies that he met her the previous day and reveals the circumstances under which they met, the tension between mother and son escalates. After claiming simply to be "curious" about Melanie, Lydia's disapproval becomes blatant as she disparages the young woman's wealth and notoriety, especially a newspaper story about her having jumped "naked" into a fountain in Rome.

> LYDIA: It's none of my business, of course, but when you bring a girl
> like that to . . .

As Mitch stands his ground and assures her that he "can handle Melanie Daniels" by himself, the tension between them reaches a peak over what it is that Mitch desires:

> LYDIA: Well. . . . *(She sighs)* So long as you know what you want,
> Mitch.
> MITCH: I know <u>exactly</u> what I want, Mother.

Added to what we have seen and heard in the previous scene, Hunter's description of Lydia's gestures and language mirrors the classic motif of the possessive mother unwilling to let go of an unmarried son whom she depends upon for emotional support, while he is asserting both his independence and the right to define his own life as a man.

Even as the romantic comedy has become a piece of domestic melodrama, Hunter tries to retain the tone of some of their initial flirtatious banter as a way of affirming the growing love between them. At the same time, he tries to color the emerging bird attacks with contemporary political nuance, especially concerning the cold war and the ever present threat of nuclear devastation that was an undercurrent in the du Maurier story but which the director did not want in the film. After the attack down the chimney of the Brenner house, there is the scene that Hitchcock omitted from the film, which we have referred to previously, in which Hunter has Melanie facetiously claim that what the birds are doing amounts to a revolutionary insurrection. As Mitch joins in the banter, the two of them come closer romantically.

> MELANIE: . . . *(Pause; then sagely)* I think I've got it all figured out, by the way.
> MITCH: Really? Tell me about it.
> MELANIE: *(Secretively)* It's an uprising.
> MITCH: Of birds?
> MELANIE: Certainly, of birds.
> Mitch grins.
> MELANIE (Cont'd): It all started several months ago with a peasant sparrow up in the hills, a malcontent. He went around telling all the other sparrows that human beings weren't fit to rule this planet, preaching wherever anyone would listen. . . .
> MITCH: Growing a beard. . . .
> MELANIE: *(Delighted)* Yes, of course, he <u>had</u> to have a beard! "Birds of the world, unite!" he kept saying over and over . . .
> MITCH: So they united.
> . . .
> MELANIE: . . . eventually, even the more serious-minded birds began to listen. Why <u>should</u> humans rule? They asked themselves.
> MITCH: Hear!
> MELANIE: Why <u>should</u> we submit ourselves to their domination?
> MITCH: Hear, hear!
> MELANIE: And all the while, that sparrow was getting in his little messages. Birds of the world, unite!
> MITCH: Take wing!
> MELANIE: You have nothing to lose but your feathers.

A moment later, their conversation turns serious as Melanie expresses her fear of what is happening, and exclaims: "Oh damn it, why did you have to walk into that shop?" Then, Hunter's directions indicate, "They kiss suddenly and fiercely." The kiss signifies their acknowledgment of their emotional and erotic bond, and Hunter artfully prepares us for it with the comic dialogue initiated by Melanie. It is as if the romantic comedy begun in the pet shop culminates at the very moment the characters and the narrative turn darkly serious, and now the melodramatic terror of the birds attacking children at a birthday party replaces comedy, which was Hunter's original intention. Further, Melanie's description of the sparrow revolutionary from the hills who sports a beard, as Mitch insists, and spouts Marxist rhetoric, has overtones of Fidel Castro—a bearded Marxist from the rural Cuban hills who came to power in the period the film was produced, and who was dramatically connected to the fragility of the world nuclear situation, a theme Hunter would attempt to pick up later. Thus, love is blossoming in the narrative against the symbolic backdrop of references to a world situation that the audience was all too familiar with, one that would be pushed to the brink by the Cuban Missile Crisis a few months before the film's release. So Hunter has given the comedy and the emerging eros here a darker, more urgent context.

Writing in 1962, Hunter was clearly influenced by another contemporary figure, John F. Kennedy. Like the young president, who was credited with protecting the security of the nation, especially during the Missile Crisis, Mitch, as Hunter describes him, can handle the toughest hoods just as we see he can fight off the most vicious birds to protect his loved ones when necessary. And like the handsome Kennedy, who was consistently portrayed as a committed, loving husband and doting father to a young family, Mitch is dedicated to, and even indulgent of, his young sister and mother, having willingly assumed the mantle of his dead father. In this sense, the image that Mitch presents approaches more closely the contemporary stereotypical ideal than that of any of the other male protagonists in Hitchcock films of the previous decade. Hunter has created a knightly Mitch, strong, capable, authoritative, and protective. He neither boasts nor exhibits any bravado as he takes charge of situations, and he can be thoughtful and caring when the occasion demands. It is not difficult to see why he is so attractive to Melanie Daniels and Annie Hayworth, or why his mother is so attached to him and depends on him so much.

The personal similarities between Mitch and Kennedy are striking. Mitch is a well-dressed, even stylish patrician. He and his family appear to be gentry in their community, particularly among the Bodega Bay farmers and fishermen. A successful San Francisco lawyer and urbanite during the week, he is respected and admired by the local merchants, farmers, and fisherman in the town where he weekends in a manner that is reminiscent of the aristocratic Kennedy's common touch with ordinary folk. Like the young president, who was seen sailing at his family's compound in Hyannis Port, Mitch's homestead is in a remote nautical locale with its own dock. Even the language Hunter gives him has overtones of Kennedy's. At the Tides Restaurant during the bird attack on the town, he admonishes the fishing-boat captain that they have to get Bodega Bay "on the move" if they are to prevail against the creatures. During his 1960 campaign, Kennedy told audiences that America needed to get "on the move again" to contrast himself with his opponent, Richard Nixon, and the Eisenhower-era polices that Nixon had helped design. In fact, one of Kennedy's campaign themes was ending the "complacency" the United States had fallen into, which, he asserted, was preventing it from making the tough decisions and taking the courageous action that the times demanded. Obviously, there are differences in degree and in context, but the parallels are informative, especially when we look at Mitch's character in this context.

Further, Kennedy's public persona as a family man was crucial to his personal popularity during both his election campaign and his presidency. Interestingly, while Melanie and Mitch have become a couple at this point in the narrative, Hunter's primary interest is in the nascent family that develops through the course of the screenplay. As is clear in the scene between the two women, Melanie, through her bond with him, also bonds with Mitch's family, represented here by Lydia, his mother. At this point, Hunter's stage directions and dialogue extend the earlier motifs of loneliness and isolation that surround Annie to the older woman and her possessiveness. His directions describe Lydia's room as "cluttered with the mementos of a life no longer valid. There are photographs of her dead husband, souvenirs of trips taken together, bric-a-brac of Mitch's childhood." Lydia reveals her vulnerability and fears to Melanie and in so doing creates a bridge between the two of them where formerly there had been only distance and wariness:

> LYDIA: I lost my husband four years ago, you know. *(Pause)* It's odd how you depend on someone for strength, and then suddenly all the strength is gone, and you're alone . . .

Hunter's directions focus on the emotional resonance of the lines and a beginning of an affinity between the two women:

> *A curious thing is happening in this room. Lydia, for perhaps the first time since her husband's death, is discussing it with another person. Curiously, the person is* Melanie.

LYDIA: *(Honestly and simply)* I miss him. . . . Cathy's a child you
   know, and Mitch . . . *(She shrugs a little sadly)* . . . Mitch has his
   own life. . . .

After admitting how little she knows about Melanie, whom she realizes
Mitch is connecting with "in his own life," Lydia adds that she doesn't
know how she feels about her but wants to like any girl her son chooses,
fearing that a breach with him over this woman would increase her isolation and loneliness: "You see, I . . . wouldn't want to be left alone. I don't
think I could bear being left alone."

This fear of isolation and of the unknown is further developed in the
later Tides Restaurant scene, where both fears are extended to the whole
town. Hunter added this scene to explore the bird attacks in broader
human terms and their impact not simply on individuals or families, but
on a whole community. The scene explores varying perspectives on the
attacks that reveal the inadequacy of all human explanations—including
logical and scientific ones—as well as the futility of resistance. There
is Mrs. Bundy, the ornithologist and skeptical scientist who doubts the
very possibility of what the birds have supposedly done; the drunk who
keeps quoting the Bible and declares that it is "the end of the world";
the salesman who takes a bellicose position and urges everyone to fight
back and kill every bird possible; the mother who simply wants to escape
and protect her two children; and Deke Carter, the restaurant owner
and his wife Helen, the waitress, who, like Sholes, the fishing captain,
are at a loss about what it all means and how to respond. Mitch, who
wants them all to join together and take direct, united action, comes as
close as the screenplay does to defining what is happening in symbolic
or existential terms:

MITCH: *(Flatly)* I think we're in trouble. I don't know how or why
   this started, but I know it's here and I know we'd be crazy to
   ignore it. . . . *(Exploding)*
   Yes, the bird war, the bird attack, the bird plague, you call it
   what you want to, they're out there massing someplace and
   they'll be back, you can count on that! (Emphasis added)

Perhaps the most important function of the Tides Restaurant scene is to
bring the community of Bodega Bay into the narrative to show simultane-

ously how crucial the larger idea of community is to human survival and how community fails here as the citizens are unable to unite and work together in the face of the destruction, hysteria, and chaos unleashed by the birds, despite the urging of Mitch. For community, like the couple and the family, is at the heart of what the finished film suggests is needed for human endurance and fulfillment, even more than erotic love, and perhaps this is the reason why Hitchcock cut the romantic kiss between Mitch and Melanie but allowed most of this scene to remain intact.

While much is the same, there are several other differences between the film and the final screenplay in regard to this scene. In the screenplay, gulls smash through a window in the restaurant at one point, and at another point a man fires at them with a rifle. The script also contains several shots of Mitch rescuing a child from the window of a burning building that do not appear in the film. More crucially, there is no scene in the script like the one in the film in which the mother of the two children attacks Melanie as the cause of the bird violence and then is slapped by her; instead, after the assault upon the town, the woman screams at Mrs. Bundy, who mutters some vague explanation and stares off uncomprehendingly in the distance. Presumably Hitchcock added the somewhat shocking verbal assault on Melanie and the subsequent slap not to imply that Melanie's arrival in Bodega Bay did indeed instigate the bird attacks but to show how difficult it is to sustain a community during traumatic times and to reinforce the idea that the attacks are a proving ground for her to overcome her earlier shallowness and immaturity and to gain the self-confidence to become an integral part of the Brenner family.

Melanie's arrival at the Tides Restaurant just before the birds attack again marks a new stage in her development as a strong, resourceful person in her own right. In fact, in this and in the subsequent scene where the family is besieged at the Brenner house, Melanie appears to have gained a more mature outlook on things as she calls on the Brenners' neighbors in the Tides to recognize just how awful their predicament is, and in the following scene she ably helps Mitch to fortify the house. Hunter tries to indicate this in the stage directions, which describe her soiled fashionable clothing and her "weary wisdom" and "strength." This strength and resolve, Melanie's growth as a self-reliant person, is carried into the scene of the attack upon the house.

As the family gathers wood to secure the windows and doors, and Melanie and Mitch become closer, the two of them observe the lovebirds tweeting. In the background on the radio a news story from San Francisco mentions the attack on the school children at Bodega Bay and ends with the actual voice of John F. Kennedy delivering the conclusion of his 1962 State of the Union Address, where he refers to America's place in the precarious world situation. In addition to the obvious threat of nuclear war, which Kennedy alludes to, the president underscores the theme of people working together and of the necessity of community as he refers to the "free community of nations" and the "family of man." Meanwhile, the Brenner family and its new recruit Melanie are working closely together to survive rather than as isolated individuals, with the young woman playing a crucial role. She and Mitch embrace again in a reaffirmation of their affection, and she declares, "I don't want to be safe. I want to be with you," revealing how profoundly her priorities have changed and she has grown.

After the bird assault upon her in the attic, Mitch drives the family through the devastated town where they come to a perilous crossroad. It is Melanie who makes the decision that they risk driving through the birds, since it is their only chance to get to San Francisco and safety. The directions begin:

> *There is a long silence. It is Melanie who has the strongest reason for fearing the birds. It is Melanie . . . who makes the decision.*
> MELANIE: Then go ahead, Mitch.

It is with this tone of hope that Hunter concludes the screenplay as the car escapes the town and outruns the birds. As his directions indicate,

> *There is hope in their faces as the car streaks into the wind. Not a wild exuberance, but a relaxation of tension.*

And they continue forward into the "sudden sunrise ahead."

Marnie

Like *Psycho*, *Marnie* is an exploration of a criminal sexual pathology that is the result of individual and cultural repression, major preoccupations of American cultural critics of its contemporary period. Even more explicitly than *Psycho*, *Marnie* focuses on female sexuality. However, the film was far less culturally groundbreaking than *Psycho*, with its frank opening scene and shocking portrayal of a murderous psychosis. It links Marnie's pathology and criminality directly to inadequate, even harmful mothering, which has left her both a criminal and a sexually frigid woman who exploits the very men whom she cannot stand to touch her. To make this character explicable and to facilitate her healing, Jay Presson Allen's screenplay built two themes into the narrative, each of which is related to a different school of contemporary psychology or psychotherapy.[6] The first is the psychoanalytic insight that bringing to consciousness a repressed traumatic memory can heal a disturbed psyche; the second, which emerges from Mark's language, is an analogy between human behavior and animal instinct that appears in the film's hunting/trapping/ zoology subtext.

Allen introduced the script with lengthy, elaborate character descriptions of Marnie and Mark that read like the kind of character introduction Eugene O'Neill favored in his long plays of the 1920s, when he assumed that more people would read his plays than watch them on the stage. Here is the first paragraph of her description of Mark:

MARK RUTLAND *is the American equivalent of an aristocrat. That is to say he has the rather uncommon twentieth-century grace of identity. He is, however, too intelligent to settle for this. He has probably always been in rebellion against his stultifying background, but his kindness and generous insight would have, of necessity, made this rebellion a quiet, insidious sluffing off of classic traditions and lines of thought.*

And of Marnie:

MARNIE EDGAR *is twenty-five years old; she has a delicate blonde beauty and a controlled, soft-spoken manner that enables her to pass for a lady. Her intelligence and humor are quick, but she has little insight into herself or others. Relying rather too much on the swiftness of her intelligence, she is likely to act on impulse.*

It is difficult to speculate on what Hitchcock thought of this literary language, with its emphasis on characteristics that are too subtly particularized to be captured by the camera. One imagines that he simply ignored the descriptions completely, assuming that if they helped Allen write the screenplay, so be it. But they also must have indicated to him that the screenplay would undoubtedly be overwritten, which it was: much of the work he did with Allen subsequent to the first scenario she submitted was simply to cut dramatically. This was Allen's first screenplay, after all. Hitchcock was extremely fond of her, and they appeared to share the same conception of the film. But he realized that a playwright who was a novice screenwriter would rely too much on dialogue and too little on visual imagery. Instead of criticism, his experience and tact led him to give her guidance and instruction.

The first draft, submitted in early August, was 248 pages long. The final draft, submitted in October after several meetings between Allen and Hitchcock, was 219 pages, still overly long. Perhaps this is why the scene Evan Hunter had created, based on a scene from the novel in which Marnie steals the money from a safe at a movie theater, and which for some reason remained in all of Allen's drafts even though she hadn't written it, was either not filmed or was later cut. (In the script the scene runs for seven pages.) Or perhaps Hitchcock cut the scene because it delays the first meeting between Marnie and Mark, a relationship that, in the film, is more central to the story than it is in the novel. Indeed, the novel is appropriately titled, while the film might have been more justifiably called "Marnie and Mark."

The fact that the character description of Mark is much longer than that of Marnie, and that it ends with the remark, "He is a *hero,* for chrissake," shows that Allen approached the screenplay with the assumption that she had two protagonists to develop, not only the eponymous one. She and Hitchcock had agreed to cut the other two male figures in the novel, as discussed in the previous chapter, which made it necessary that the Mark Rutland character take on much more of the story's masculine presence. (Again, casting Sean Connery in the role at the beginning of his James Bond fame also required more script attention to Mark.)

Hitchcock left in long, novelistic descriptions of the settings, presumably because they demonstrate that Allen could think in terms of mise-en-scène, though many of them are still more appropriate for the stage: "In the living room [of Mrs. Edgar's house] there are doilies and meager but carefully nurtured pot-plants of the African violet variety. The mantel and cupboard shelves are repositories for pridefully displayed bits of bad china . . . cups, plates, figurines. The only book in the living room is a Bible which lies open on a table near the window. There are two pictures on the walls, Landseer's *Dignity and Impudence* and Millet's *The Angelus.*

Wherever in the room a bit of metal shows, it is polished to a regimental sheen." The detailed, specific description is remarkably reminiscent of Ibsen's stage directions for the living rooms of his petit-bourgeois characters.

Allen's script varies considerably from Evan Hunter's final draft, Joseph Stefano's treatment, and Winston Graham's novel. As late as April 1963, Hitchcock fully intended to use Hunter's script—with the significant exception of his "honeymoon" scene that omitted the "rape." Yet once he fired Hunter and moved on to Allen, he was obviously prepared to make a number of crucial changes to the story as script development proceeded. The director approved a major expansion of the role of Mark, the removal of the characters Terry and Dr. Roman, the addition of Lil, and still one more alteration of the content of the primal scene that caused Marnie Edgar's severe neurosis. In other words, Hitchcock and his newly hired writer decided to depart extensively from the novel's plot and characterization as late as the summer before preproduction began and after three years of work on the scenario that had been consistent with the basic narrative strategies of the source novel.

Was this decision wise from an aesthetic perspective? On the one hand, increasing Mark's importance and dropping the other two main male characters detracts from the centrality of Marnie's dilemma and puts more of the focus on Mark and his own neuroses. His gentrified background also moves the script much further from the novel's "angry young woman" tone and atmosphere and makes one of its primary settings this upscale world where Marnie is herself a more gentrified character. On the other hand, only a larger part would have attracted an actor of Sean Connery's box-office reputation, and indeed the role Allen wrote for him makes Mark Rutland a more interesting and complex character than he is in the novel. And the Rutland world gives this film the very touches of Hitchcockian glamour that *Psycho* lacked and that *The Birds* dispenses with once the birds begin to attack.

To develop the characters of Marnie and Mark and the psychological dynamics of their relationship, Allen created a specific imagery that dominates the dialogue that Mark speaks. The animal imagery that characterizes Allen's script, as opposed to Hunter's, works so well precisely because Mark's role is more central to the film's concerns. The imagery links the two characters: Allen presents Mark, the zoologist, as a hunter, and Marnie as his prey. In the finished script, Mark and Marnie discuss a photograph of a "snarling jungle cat" in his office:

MARNIE: Goodness! What is that dangerous looking animal?
MARK: Sophie? She's a jaguarondi. I had her in South America a few
years ago. *(With some pride)* I trained her.
MARNIE: Oh—what did you train it to do?
MARK: To trust me.
MARNIE: Is that all?
MARK: That is a great deal . . . for a jaguarondi.

And, of course, for most of the remainder of the script that is exactly what Mark tries to achieve with Marnie. In her first draft, Allen had included the following statement:

MARK: . . . passionate . . . jaguarundis cannot be bent or broken. If you menace them, they become even more menacing. If they're mishandled. . . . Well, like many wild things, their final sanctuary is voluntary death.

A few lines later Mark identifies himself as a zoologist and informs Marnie that "[l]ady animals figure very largely as predators," which he has called "the criminal class of the animal world." Pointedly, Mark Rutland is setting up instinctual zoological models for himself and Marnie: he casts himself as a hunter who is attempting to trap a wild, deadly animal. Marnie does not reject this characterization of her situation. According to Allen's directions, "She does not pick up the challenge, only smiles vaguely." Her evasiveness, of course, is one of her principal tools for survival in the jungle that is the world from her damaged perspective.

The animal motif gives Allen's script a consistently behaviorist approach to Mark's and Marnie's psychological makeups, one that fits rather uneasily within the generally Freudian character structure that Winston Graham had introduced and Hunter had followed. Although Mark strongly recommends that Marnie read Jung's *The Undiscovered Self,* which, despite some major differences from psychoanalysis, certainly accepts Freud's idea that the unconscious mind controls our decision making, Allen's imagery focuses on our animal instincts as the determining factor and does not relegate these instincts to unconscious recesses of the psyche—indeed, Mark is aware that he is excited by the thought of trapping and taming this female he has found. Simply put, the difference between the two characters in the script is that Mark is conscious of his instincts and what they drive him to do, while Marnie, due to her repression of her childhood trauma, has not yet learned how her rational thoughts are based on primitive impulses. Allen nods in the direction of psychoanalysis by including the free-association game in the scene in which Mark recommends Jung's book. A more extended use of free association is employed by Dr. Roman in the novel, and Allen clearly modeled the scene on this part of the book. However, the removal of Dr. Roman and thus the analytic sessions that are crucial to Marnie's development in Graham's book, and their replacement by this brief interlude in which Mark tries to play doctor, ultimately diminishes the Freudian influence. In fact, Hitchcock acknowledged to Truffaut that they had "simplified the . . . psychoanalysis."[7] When the content of the original trauma is revealed at the end, its oedipal nature seems arbitrary instead of satisfying, somewhat like the psychiatrist's "explanation" of Norman's behavior at the end of *Psycho*.

On another level, Mark the therapist has contemporary "political" connections to Mitch, another powerful, protective male. One element in the film that is related to these historical developments is its representation of his loving and protective side. On one level, Mark seems a continuation and intensification of the portrait of Mitch Brenner in *The Birds,* with his energetic, assertive, take-charge, Kennedyesque masculinity. But Mark, the principal male character in the film, is a more potent and effectual male presence than Mitch. He is in every sense more like the vigorous, activist Kennedy who defeated Stevenson and several other rivals to win the nomination in 1960, whose tough-minded Ivy League liberalism he seems to share. In fact, in lines dropped from the final Allen screenplay, Dad disparagingly remarks that Mark went "to Columbia University in New York," and Lil adds that he is "a registered Democrat."

Once Mark "captures" Marnie after she robs the Rutland safe, Allen specifically develops the animal and hunting imagery that was introduced during the storm scene in Mark's office. As they are driving in Mark's car, Allen's directions indicate that "[Marnie] has no time to think, only blind instinct drives her to fight the net she feels slipping over her." When Mark claims that he is in love with her, in the screenplay Marnie describes her feelings in dialogue in which she becomes a captured animal:

MARNIE: *(Her voice is low, almost a hiss of accusation)* You don't love me. . . . I'm just something you've . . . caught. . . . You think I'm some kind of animal you've trapped!

MARK: That's right. You are. And I've caught something <u>really</u> wild this time, haven't I?

MARNIE: *(Bursts out)* Go buy yourself a God-damned zoo! <u>Let me go!</u>

MARK: *(Shakes his head)* I've tracked you and caught you, and by God, I'm going to keep you.

Her use of animal imagery is Allen's most distinctive literary contribution to the three-year development of the script. She and the director together decided to enhance the role of Mark, but it was the writer who added the hunter/prey motif. It adds a dark psychological aura to the motivations of Mark Rutland, and it increases our sympathy for Marnie, two developments Hitchcock was clearly pleased by.

Perhaps the scene that most effectively incorporates the theme of the hunt and the behaviorist/instinct-oriented psychology that dominates the script is the shipboard "honeymoon" scene. Here Allen presents the first nights of Mark and Marnie's marriage as a game in which the trapped prey refuses to be subdued or tamed by her captor, until he forcibly compels her to submit. The language Allen uses in the stage directions describes a cagelike prison: "Marnie cannot decide where to move . . . in which direction safety might lie"; "Like a prisoner responding to a warden's order . . ."; "She, like a cornered animal, glares back at him." The dialogue in this sequence is extremely blunt, the beginning of the last sentence so graphic that it had to be omitted from the film:

MARK (Cont'd): Eventually you'd have got caught . . . by somebody. You're such a tempting little thing. Some other . . . *(a faint smile)* sexual blackmailer . . . would have got his hands on you. . . . The chances of it being someone as "permissive" as me are pretty remote. Sooner or later you'd have gone to jail or onto your back across an office desk with some angry old bull of a businessman taking what he figured was coming to him.

The animal references become shockingly callous when Mark tells Marnie about his mother: "When I was six weeks old she turned me over to a nurse and rejoined the hunt. She must have been feeling enormously liberated that morning. She outstripped not only the other riders but the hounds as well. She passed the hunt; she passed the pack; she overtook the bloody fox itself, and her horse tripped over it . . . *(dramatic pause)* I was the only boy in my crowd whose mother was buried in her boots." Marnie looks at him with "narrow-eyed suspicion" after this speech over dinner: would a man this irreverent toward his own dead mother keep his word that he will not "handle" her any more on this voyage?

As the days pass, Mark steadfastly maintains his optimism that this ill-matched marriage can be successful, but to do so he again takes refuge in the logic of natural selection, not human will. At night he reads books on "some obscure zoological subject" and on entomology. He tells Marnie, "Don't underestimate yourself. The human animal has long since proved its genius for adaptation. You can be anything you want." When she sneers at the idea that she could become a "society hostess," Mark replies, "If you fancy yourself presiding over a salon, I'm sure you'll do it well. . . . After all, the one to whom we owe the most . . . that fish . . . the one that managed to find its painful way out of the water onto the land . . . let's face it . . . [was] a social climber." Connecting zoological and social evolution in this dialogue that was omitted from the film, Mark insists that Marnie, the trapped animal, can evolve into the matriarch of her cage.

Mark's analysis of Marnie in terms of Darwinian survival of the fittest culminates in his final speech about the "singularity" of all the individual elements of nature. It is a fine speech for a play, though it is somewhat surprising that Hitchcock retained it instead of using an image to replace it:

> MARK (Cont'd): In Africa . . . in Kenya . . . there's quite a beautiful flower . . . coral colored with little green-tipped blossoms rather like a hyacinth. But if you reach out to touch it you will discover that the flower is not a flower at all. It's a design made up of hundreds of tiny insects called Fattid bugs. They escape the eyes of hungry birds by living and dying in the shape of a flower . . . a flower, incidentally, the Fattid bug seems to have invented, as there is none other like it in nature. Even the flower the bugs imitate is singular.

Finally, later that night, a drunken and frustrated Mark forces Marnie to submit to him. It is as if the lion tamer has concluded that violence is necessary to keep his prize in captivity.

Allen's use of imagery is supported by, and might even have been suggested by, the fox hunt itself, which leads to Marnie's shooting of Forio.

Shortly before the hunt scene there is a tense, hostile exchange between Lil and Marnie, during which Lil offers her money to simply leave Mark. When Marnie refuses, the scene ends with Lil going back to the house to call Strutt and begin Marnie's public exposure as a compulsive thief. Lil, of course, wants Marnie out of the way to have Mark for herself, and thus she too uses predatory language in the screenplay that never made its way into the film: when Marnie tells Lil that she is somewhat frightened of the actual killing of the fox, Lil retorts, "Really? Killing is my very favorite thing! *(Laughs)* Until I was fourteen I wanted to go to Kenya and join the Mau Mau." And later, "You really should consider the offer. Because I do plan to get rid of you, you know. One way or another."

During the hunt scene Allen's stage directions are replete with the imagery she has used to describe Mark and Marnie's relationship: the "snarling hounds tearing their quarry to pieces"; "Marnie in a rising panic identifies wholly with the fox. She feels herself surrounded by a mob of cheerful killers." Her repulsion from this bloodthirsty scene leads her to gallop away from the killing, only to cause Forio finally to crash and fall. When Lil, in what may be at least partially a moment of empathy, volunteers to shoot the fatally wounded horse instead of Marnie, the latter retorts, "viciously," "You still in the mood for killing? Didn't you get your fill back there? Wasn't there enough blood to satisfy you, Lil?" Marnie shoots Forio to put him out of his misery, a love killing as opposed to the rapacious rampage she has just witnessed.

Allen also altered Hunter's ending, in which Marnie is compelled to re-call the killing of the sailor by her mother, although that ending reflected the novel's ending more closely—in the novel, Marnie's mother *does* kill someone: her newborn infant. Hunter and Hitchcock had decided that having the mother kill an adult male (a father figure) rather than a baby she was ashamed of having given birth to made more psychological sense, and an analyst Hunter consulted concurred.[8] (In addition, killing a baby, even as background information, might have been too shocking a crime for the film's Bernice to have committed.) But in Allen's screenplay it is Marnie who killed the sailor, which is not conducive to exemplifying Freudian theory but certainly throws the spotlight on the power of violent survival instincts in Marnie, this time not turned on herself but on another. Allen nods in the direction of popularizations of Freud again when Bernice alludes to Marnie's repression of the primal scene: "I thought that when she lost the memory of that night, it was a sign of God's forgiveness. I thought I was being given another chance . . . to change everything . . . make it all up to her." When Marnie learns that her mother had told the police that she, not Marnie, "killed the sailor in self-defense," she says, "You must have loved me. . . . You must have loved me."

Thus, Marnie's full access to the hidden memory is "therapeutic" in several ways: it leads Marnie to understand that, despite her coldness, Bernice truly did love her; it explains this coldness through Bernice's acknowledgment of and guilt for her sexual past, what she calls "the fever in your body"; and it apparently has caused Marnie to feel the appeal of Mark's empathy and warmth. But from an oedipal perspective it explains little: Marnie has no unresolved Electra complex that compels her to fight her mother for a father's love. Instead, she is always trying to buy her mother's love with gifts. Mark now hopes that Marnie can allow herself to feel and act upon her sexual desires, like any healthy animal, something her repressed traumatic memory has prevented her from achieving.

Did the screenwriters write for Hitchcock in ways that suited his own particular visual style? For example, did they create a style of dialogue, as well as a system of stage directions, that would reinforce the director's predilection for the subjective camera and point-of-view editing? What we have discussed in this chapter supports an affirmative answer. All three writers, in creating the dialogue for their protagonists, did so with the intent of revealing the character's internal conflicts and not merely to create suspense or provide exposition. For example, in *The Birds,* the scene between Melanie and Lydia after the latter's visit to Dan Fawcett's farm does little to create a sense of impending terror or to set up one of the bird attacks: on the contrary, the birds have already attacked, and no further attack is imminent, so the intimate exchange between mother and potential daughter-in-law serves only to project the vulnerability of one of the two characters and the growing empathy of the other. Likewise, the scene in which Mark takes Marnie to the racetrack could be considered a "no-scene" scene, since it does nothing to further the plot and seems simply to delay Marnie's robbery of Rutland's. However, the dialogue reveals much about Marnie's hidden past, solidifies her intense love of horses, which will play an important role later in the film, and also demonstrates Mark's growing interest in and determination to uncover her unexplained fears and aberrant behavior. And in *Psycho,* Marion's desperate journey to her lover in California, during which nothing "happens" outwardly except her driving, interrupted only by the prying policeman and the hurried transaction at the used-car dealership, is presented through the complex use of voiceover and shot/reverse shot editing that precisely conveys her anxiety, her undeniable sense of satisfaction, and her guilt—emotions that are crucial to our understanding of her fragile state of mind when she encounters Norman Bates.

As for stage directions, the various drafts show how many visual descriptions, particularly point-of-view shots, Hitchcock asked the writers to add as they revised. But even the first drafts reveal a remarkable attention to visual detail that reflects internal tension. At times the character descriptions verge on the novelistic, particularly in the case of Jay Presson Allen, but always the attention to physical appearance is accompanied by a statement about exactly what character trait this outward look signifies.

The subjective approach to narrative filmmaking, which Hitchcock took further than any other contemporary American film director, enabled him to create "character" films rather than merely "situation" films—the distinction he made in his conversations with Truffaut. Not that plots are unimportant in these films, but instead of dominating the narrative strategies Hitchcock and his writers employed, they subserve the development of complex protagonists whose reactions to their environments in moments of crisis dictate the unfolding of the story's events. Stefano, Hunter, and Allen intuitively understood what their employer wanted, and knowing his visual style as well as they did from having seen many of his best films, they adapted their own talent for revealing a character's drives and motivations through dialogue, directions, and action to fit the range and power of Hitchcock's camera. The result was the last great period of Hitchcock's career.

Afterword

When their work on their respective screenplays was completed and the director had the shooting script, for all intents and purposes each screenwriter was done with the film. Hilton Green, who had been assistant director on *Psycho* and unit manager on *Marnie,* said that he recalled who the writers on those films were, but once production began it was their shooting scripts that mattered, and they were "out of the picture," although all three did come to the set on several occasions and offer "suggestions." At least at one point when they were on the set, both Hunter and Stefano voiced objections to the director at what they saw: Stefano to the some of the changes to and omissions from his script, or to what had been originally filmed, especially to the cutting of a poignant shot of the dead Marion draped over the tub with her buttocks exposed after her murder;[1] Hunter to the addition of an abandoning mother for Melanie to the dialogue during the dune scene. By contrast, Allen did manage to get some of her suggestions listened to during the filming of *Marnie,* and she was also consulted during the editing process.[2] But once the films were completed and released, each writer became essentially a critical audience member. Stefano was impressed by the suspense and shock of *Psycho* but somewhat disappointed that a few of what he considered key lines had not been included in the final cut. Hunter was disappointed at the Museum of Modern Art premiere by how consciously "arty" *The Birds* seemed to him and that his conclusion had been cut and replaced by an abrupt ending, the ambiguity of which did not seem to work. And Allen was caught up in the generally negative reviews that *Marnie* received; she essentially agreed that it was inferior Hitchcock and believed that much of the fault was hers as an inexperienced screenwriter. But with time, the early assessments of the three changed.

Stefano did not recall watching *Psycho* again until ten years after its release, when he went to see it at a Los Angeles revival house with his wife Marilyn and some friends and was struck by its brilliance and depth. For years he was ambivalent about whether it was a good career move to have written it, since the film led him to be typecast as a writer who specialized in the dark side of human experience. He had worked on the treatment of *Marnie* with Hitchcock in 1961, but in 1962 he declined Hitchcock's offer to write the screenplay since he was already creating *The Outer Limits* for television; the same year he also took umbrage when Hitchcock tried to loan him out to Columbia Pictures to satisfy the writer's contractual obligation, a gesture that effectively ended their relationship. In the following years, however, he was acutely conscious that the director's films from *Marnie* on did not fare well with critics or audiences. When he would run into members of Hitchcock's staff, such as Peggy Robertson, he would feel a sense of regret and at times a pang of guilt at not working with him again. For the rest of his life he remembered working with Hitchcock with great fondness, as well as the time he spent socializing with him. One of his favorite memories was of the director and Alma coming to his and Marilyn's Christmas party at their Beverly Hills home in 1959. Hitchcock stood in front of their piano the entire night in a prepossessing pose that seemed to announce who he was to the guests. Initially the writer had not invited him because he was told that Hitchcock rarely attended such events, but Hitchcock had heard about the party one day and asked Stefano why he hadn't been invited, and Stefano immediately insisted that he attend. As thank-you gifts, he sent the Stefanos a case of vintage wine and a French cook book. Neither of the Stefanos was much of a wine lover, but they did appreciate the book and the gesture, which they saw as Hitchcock's way of sharing a part of himself with them. Alma also bought a Christmas gift for Dominick, their young son.

Interestingly, Stefano, who had refused to write *The Birds,* with its science-fiction and horror overtones, developed a reputation for both genres through the rest of his career in film and television, sometimes in ways that seemed to parallel, or mimic, what he had written for Hitchcock. His writing over the next three decades abounds in murder, vengeance, incest, terrifying animals, and even reanimation. *Two Bits* (1995), which tells the story of a child's love for the movies while growing up in a South Philadelphia Italian-American family, is a notable exception. But he was most proud of the work he had done to create, produce, and write *The Outer Limits* in 1963 and 1964, especially his use of the show's science-fiction format to create fables about cold-war political intrigue and manipulation, specifically the darker forces underlying the irresponsible governmental authority that controls, and often destroys, people's lives. He also returned to *Psycho* in 1990 when he wrote the screenplay for the third sequel, *Psycho IV: The Beginning,* which featured Anthony Perkins in the title role and Hilton Green as executive producer and told the story of Norman's childhood and detailed his troubled relationship with Mother.

In the last decade and a half of his life, Stefano became something of an educator, mentoring film students from California universities, such as UCLA, and giving numerous talks on his collaboration with Hitchcock and on his career. He appeared on several DVDs of the director's films commenting on Hitchcock, including *Psycho* and *Marnie,* as well as programs on science fiction and television. He also received screenplay credit for Gus Van Sant's literal remake of *Psycho* in 1999 but was disappointed with Van Sant's refusal to revise and update the script. Being recognized for the excellence of his *Psycho* screenplay by the Writer's Guild was important to him, an opportunity for acknowledgment that had not come at the time when he wrote the film. As indicated above, at the end of his life he was working on a play, "Psycho/Analysis," which dramatized the period of his life when he worked on *Psycho,* when he went from a daily 9:00 A.M. appointment with his analyst to his 10:30 studio meetings with Hitchcock. Detailing the congruence of his therapy sessions, with their psychological intensity, and the artistic and personal intensity of his working sessions with the director, Stefano reveals how aspects of his own psychic life provided raw material for his depictions of Marion and Norman. In addition, he made a point of defining what he had learned from Hitchcock. At one point, he has the director say that what the audience does or doesn't see is his department, while the characters, the credibility of the story, and the dialogue are the writer's. This idea is closely related to something Stefano told us in one of our meetings. He said that one day, when they were struggling over some issue in the screenplay, Hitchcock stopped speaking and wrote him a note in which he summed up the art of film narrative: "Always trust the audience."

While Evan Hunter would have agreed that anticipating the audience's reaction animated Hitchcock's idea of film narrative, he always remained disappointed with what the director had done with, and to, his screenplay for *The Birds.* In fact, he felt that as production advanced, Hitchcock decided to appeal to a different, more artistically sophisticated, audience interested in "themes" and "ambiguity," and that this undercut what the film should have been. He consistently denied that *The Birds* had any significance beyond an intention to terrorize the audience with technical brilliance and maintained that his screenplay was originally intended simply to facilitate this goal. This was his position in *Me and Hitch,* in our interviews, and in the talk he gave when he came to one of our film classes in the fall of 2001. He sat anonymously in the back of the room for the beginning of the three-hour session, listening to the discussion and oral reports on the film he wrote. When we finally introduced him to the startled students, he answered their questions about working with Hitchcock and writing and revising the script but adamantly rejected the theoretical ideas that they had learned from their research into Hitchcock studies. He insisted that neither he nor the director had any intentions other than to "scare the hell out of the audience," an intention that he believed was only partially realized.

We pressed Hunter in interviews to agree that meanings and ideas can emerge from characterizations that a screenplay develops and from dialogue without their being preplanned conceptually. He responded by saying that when he wrote serious fiction as Evan Hunter, such a process was inevitable and thought-out, but that when he wrote an 87th Precinct novel as Ed McBain he intended only to thrill and entertain the audience using the generic expectations he was working within. *The Birds,* for Hunter, fell into the McBain category: he insisted that he and Hitchcock were initially interested only in such thrills and entertainment, and he dismissed attempts to uncover deeper levels of meaning, or of psychological and cultural significance, within it. These came later, he reiterated, both from a director anxious for artistic credibility and academics convinced that these deeper levels were there.

Hunter expressed even greater disappointment with *Marnie* and insisted that its negative critical reception made him feel badly for Hitchcock at the time and far outweighed any resentment he might have felt for being dismissed over the disputed "rape" scene. When the film was released, he had appealed to the Writer's Guild for co-credit for the screenplay, since so much of it seemed to him to echo his ideas and lines, but he eventually decided to drop this appeal. Even so, he hoped to work again with the director, and some time later, when he and his wife Anita went to dinner with the Hitchcocks in Beverly Hills, the possibility of Hunter writing for the director again came up. Yet the two never worked together again, and screenwriting did not play a large role in the rest of Hunter's career, which lasted for four more decades. He continued to write serious fiction as Evan Hunter and saw *The Blackboard Jungle* recognized in a fiftieth-anniversary edition in 2004. He also completed over fifty 87th

Precinct novels as Ed McBain, which he felt received more artistic recognition abroad than in the United States, and many of his works, including historical fiction, crime dramas, and Westerns, were adapted by others. Beyond the printed page, his greatest popular currency came from filmed versions of his 87th Precinct novels, for movies and television, particularly in Europe and Japan. One of these, Akira Kurosawa's *High Low* (1963), released the same year as *The Birds,* became one of the masterpieces of Japanese cinema. Yet he felt that the family of police he had created in these novels, and even their narrative structure, had been "copied" without attribution several times in television history, most notably in the popular *Hill Street Blues* series (1981–87).

It was Hunter who defined Hitchcock "the writer" for us, not only as the film's initiator and guide but also as a brilliant "editor" who would listen to the writer's ideas, add his own, and get the writer to think of narrative, character, dialogue, and point of view in visual terms. While he harbored some resentment for the way Hitchcock had allowed other writers such as Hume Cronyn and V. S. Pritchett to voice misgivings about characterization in *The Birds*—and even to tamper with the script, in Pritchett's case—Hunter continued to feel affection for the director and pride in having worked with him. This can be observed in several of his 87th Precinct novels in which the members of his police family make humorous references to Hitchcock films, including mocking allusions to Hunter's own work on *The Birds*. And with all of his reservations about the film, he was obviously pleased with its ongoing popularity among filmgoers and its selection as one of the ten most terrifying films of all time. When we asked him how he rated it in comparison to *North by Northwest,* he quickly replied: "It's better than *North by Northwest*!" He once even tried to interest studio executives in a sequel to *The Birds* in which Cathy (Veronica Cartwright) is all grown up, Rod Taylor and Tippi are married, and their daughter, played by Melanie Griffith, is now in love with Tom Cruise; they all must flee the Bodega Bay house as the birds attack again.[3]

Jay Presson Allen was never a champion, or even a defender, of *Marnie*. She told us that she had only seen it at its initial release, and then in an edited television showing sometime in the 1970s, and that she did not like it either time. She rated it the weakest of all of her screenplays and claimed to have no specific recollection of what she had added to the screenplay or how and why she had changed the Graham novel except in the most general sense. She faulted herself for making the script too theatrical and not cinematic enough, and for making the film too "talky" and "linear." Hitchcock, she felt, had been too uncritical of her work and the script and had not recognized how inadequate she then was to write a film of such complexity. As for the performers, she thought that Sean Connery was right for the role of Mark, "Glaswegian accent and all," but she agreed with the critics who felt that Tippi Hedren was inadequate as Marnie and lacked the acting ability to make the character real and believable. But she added that the screenplay she had written had not adequately guided the actress or conveyed the character's pathos and vulnerability. During the early 1980s and afterwards, Allen confirmed to interviewers Hedren's assertion that the director was obsessed with her, which made the experience difficult for the actress and had a negative effect on the production. At least once Allen characterized the director's relationship with the actress as Pygmalion to Galatea. With time, however, she became reluctant to discuss this aspect of the collaboration, particularly for attribution, and made us turn off the tape recorder when it came up.

Among the three writers, Allen maintained the closest personal and working relationship with Hitchcock. She had lived in the Hitchcocks' house during the time she wrote *Marnie* and came to know the director and Alma well. She considered Hitchcock a cinematic genius who had a general interest in concepts such as psychoanalysis but was "no intellectual" and had not read Freud. She also believed that he was surprisingly naïve in some ways, and much more romantic and wistful than the more grounded and perceptive Alma, whose cinematic and personal judgments he depended upon, especially where people were concerned. To follow up on what Hunter had said about the director, Allen portrayed Alma as the "editor's editor." During their collaboration, Hitchcock confided in Allen often and loved to be around her and women in general—especially strong ones over whom he had some authority, as he did over her. She and her husband Louis socialized frequently with the Hitchcocks after the film and even talked of taking a round-the-world cruise, on which they would work on a new film. But the most important follow-up to *Marnie* that Allen was involved in was the unrealized film *Mary Rose,* for which she wrote the screenplay.

Hitchcock had been fascinated by the J. M. Barrie play from the time he first saw it on the London stage in 1920, and from at least the early 1940s he had wanted to adapt it as a film. Allen began work on the project in 1964, adapting for the screen the Barrie drama about a young mother who disappears on a mysterious Scottish island only to return unchanged many years later as a ghost who encounters her grown son whom she has painfully missed for all of his life. The story possesses overtones of the otherworldly romanticism of *Vertigo,* such as the ghostly Madeleine and Scotty's love for her, and it has echoes of the poignancy of Marnie's longing for her mother's love at the end of the film when she insists: "You must have loved me!"

Before the project was quashed by Universal, Allen wrote two drafts of the screenplay, which was originally intended for Tippi Hedren. She took Barrie's material in a darker direction, foregrounding and extending the play's elements of fear, anguish, and violence.[4] More than any of his films, *Mary Rose* would have expressed the longing and wistfulness that were part of Hitchcock's nature and vision and that he could only get in touch with indirectly in his thrillers. But even with the failure of this work to get produced and the critical failure of *Marnie,* Allen felt that it was Hitchcock who gave her the fullest understanding of film, taught her how to think and write visually, and inspired her to go into a life of screenwriting: a life in which, of the three writers, she was the most successful. In addition to *The Prime of Miss Jean Brodie, Cabaret, Deathtrap,* Allen's personal favorite, *Prince of the City,* and other films, she also wrote the celebrated television show *Family,* which ran from 1976 to 1980.

After *Marnie* and his work with Allen, Hitchcock would make four more films and work with four more writers. Two of them were the accomplished screenwriters of two of his best 1950s films: Samuel Taylor would write *Topaz* (1969), and Ernest Lehman, *Family Plot* (1976). Two other writers, Brian Moore, who wrote *Torn Curtain* (1965), and Anthony Shaffer, who wrote *Frenzy* (1972), were distinguished authors in their own right, of works such as the novel *The Lonely Passion of Judith Hearne* (1955) and the play *Sleuth* (1970), respectively. Yet Hitchcock's films during these years had neither his own engagement nor the appeal to audiences that he had had earlier in his career and seemed to lack the human and artistic vision he had reached in the triptych.

All three writers looked back upon their collaboration with Hitchcock as a golden moment, a time when they had the opportunity to share and participate within a singular creative vision. Stefano felt that what he and the director achieved in *Psycho* gave him an almost impossible standard to live up to for the rest of his creative life, though one that he treasured and that continued to enrich his work and life. Hunter continued to feel a lifelong sense of accomplishment and of incompleteness about *The Birds,* of a masterful but not fully realized opportunity for himself and Hitchcock. And Allen, for all her disappointment in *Marnie,* seemed to recognize that it was more than the sum of its parts and more than just the product of her artistic immaturity: despite her reservations, she had a hand in creating a watershed moment in the director's work and in the history of cinema. For us, getting to know the three of them was a personally rich and rewarding experience and a moment inside the greatness they had witnessed and helped to create.

Notes

PREFACE

1 Walter Raubicheck and Walter Srebnick, eds., *Hitchcock's Rereleased Films: From* Rope *to* Vertigo (Detroit: Wayne State University Press, 1991).
2 Stephen Rebello, *Alfred Hitchcock and the Making of* Psycho (New York: St. Martin's Griffin, 1990); Tony Lee Moral, *Alfred Hitchcock and the Making of* Marnie (Lanham, Md.: Scarecrow Press, 2002); Dan Aulier, *Hitchcock's Notebooks* (New York: HarperCollins, 2001): Bill Krohn, *Hitchcock at Work* (London: Phaidon, 2000); Will Schmenner and Corinne Granof, *Casting a Shadow: Creating the Hitchcock Film* (Evanston, Ill.: Northwestern University Press, 2007); Steven De Rosa, *Writing with Hitchcock: The Collaboration of Alfred Hitchcock and John Michael Hayes* (New York: Faber and Faber, 1999).
3 Donald Spoto, *The Dark Side of Genius: The Life of Alfred Hitchcock* (Boston: Little, Brown, 1983).
4 David Thomson, *The Moment of* Psycho: *How Alfred Hitchcock Taught America to Love Murder* (New York: Basic Books, 2010).
5 Evan Hunter, *Me and Hitch* (New York: Faber and Faber, 1997).
6 Eric Rohmer and Claude Chabrol, *Hitchcock: The First Forty-Four Films,* trans. Stanley Hochman (New York: Frederick Unger, 1979).
7 Francois Truffaut, *Hitchcock* (New York: Touchstone Books, 1984).

CHAPTER I. THE TRIPTYCH AND THE SCREENPLAYS

1 Peter Bogdanovich and Orson Welles, *This Is Orson Welles,* ed. Jonathan Rosenbaum (New York: HarperCollins: 1992), 63.
2 Francois Truffaut, *Hitchcock* (New York: Touchstone Books, 1984), 222.
3 Ibid.; Steven Rebello, *Alfred Hitchcock and the Making of* Psycho (New York: St. Martin's Griffin, 1990), 40.
4 Patrick McGilligan, *Alfred Hitchcock: A Life in Darkness and Light* (New York: HarperCollins, 2003), 61.
5 Truffaut, *Hitchcock,* 72.
6 Alfred Hitchcock, Lecture at Columbia University, in *Hitchcock on Hitchcock: Selected Writings and Interviews,* ed. Sidney Gottlieb (Berkeley: University of California Press, 1995), 271.
7 Patricia Hitchcock O'Connell and Laurent Bouzereau, *Alma Hitchcock: The Woman Behind the Man* (New York: Berkley Books, 2003).
8 McGilligan, *Alfred Hitchcock,* 78.
9 See Charles Barr, *English Hitchcock* (Moffat, Scotland: Cameron and Hollis, 1999), 22–26, 78–81, 132–34.

10 Stannard wrote *The Pleasure Garden* (1926), *The Mountain Eagle* (1926), *The Lodger* (1926), *Downhill* (1927), *Easy Virtue* (1927), *The Farmer's Wife* (1928), *Champagne* (1928), and *The Manxman* (1929).

11 McGilligan, *Alfred Hitchcock*, 111–17.

12 Bennett wrote *The 39 Steps* (1935), *Secret Agent* (1936), *Sabotage* (1936), and *Young and Innocent* (1937).

13 Leonard Leff, *Hitchcock and Selznick: The Rich and Strange Collaboration of Alfred Hitchcock and David O. Selznick* (New York: Weidenfeld and Nicholson, 1987).

14 Ibid.

15 See McGilligan, *Alfred Hitchcock*, 331–96; Bill Krohn, *Hitchcock at Work* (New York: Phaidon, 2003), 82–103.

16 See McGilligan, *Alfred Hitchcock*, 481–82; Steven De Rosa, *Writing with Hitchcock* (New York, Faber and Faber, 2001).

17 Barr, *English Hitchcock*, 20–30, 35.

18 Samuel Taylor, "Reflections on *Vertigo*," in *Hitchcock's Rereleased Films: From Rope to Vertigo*, ed. Walter Raubicheck and Walter Srebnick (Detroit: Wayne State University Press, 1991), 288. Hitchcock characterized the short story as "the nearest art form to the motion picture" because it requires the reader "to sit down and read it in one sitting." In Budge Crawley, Fletcher Markle, and Gerald Pratley, "I Wish I Didn't Have to Shoot the Picture: An Interview with Alfred Hitchcock," in *Focus on Hitchcock*, ed. Albert J. La Valley (Englewood Cliffs, N.J.: Prentice-Hall, 1972), 25–26.

19 Taylor, "Reflections on *Vertigo*," 288.

20 Ibid.

21 Truffaut, *Hitchcock*, 103.

22 Authors' interview with Joseph Stefano, New York City, April 10, 2001.

23 Authors' interview with Evan Hunter, New York City, July 11, 2001.

24 Authors' interview with Jay Presson Allen, New York City, November 16, 2001.

25 Stefano interview.

26 Robert J. Corber approaches the connection of Hitchcock to cold-war ideology from the perspective of homophobia and emphasizes the importance of the contemporary preoccupation with mothering, sexuality, and masculinity and how it was linked to concerns about national security and subversion. While Corber does not discuss *The Birds* or *Marnie*, he argues that *Psycho* presents a subversive discourse on psychological expertise and heterosexuality. Robert J. Corber, *In the Name of National Security: Hitchcock, Homophobia, and the Political Construction of Gender in Postwar America* (Durham, N.C.: Duke University Press, 1993), 185–216.

27 Ibid., 13.

28 Barr, *English Hitchcock*, 88.

29 Robin Wood, *Hitchcock's Films Revisited,* rev. ed. (New York: Columbia University Press, 2002; originally published as *Hitchcock's Films*). Steven De Rosa also points out that Hayes brought psychological concerns to the four films he worked on (*Writing with Hitchcock,* 30–38, 123–24, 138–41, 167–69).

30 It took until 1959 for D. H. Lawrence's 1929 novel of interclass British sexuality, *Lady Chatterley's Lover,* to be published in the United States.

31 Truffaut, *Hitchcock,* 285.

32 Stefano interview.

33 Hunter interview.

34 Ibid.

35 See Michael S. Kimmel, *Manhood in America* (New York: Free Press, 1996); Tony Lee Moral, *Alfred Hitchcock and the Making of* Marnie (Lanham, Md.: Scarecrow Press, 2002), 42–43.

36 Elaine Tyler May, *Homeward Bound: American Families in the Cold War Era* (New York: Basic Books, 1988), 98–99.

37 See Wood, *Hitchcock's Films Revisited,* 388–405.

38 Allen interview.

CHAPTER 2. THE SOURCES

1 For a discussion of the idea of transformation, see James Naremore, ed., *Film Adaptation* (New Brunswick, N.J.: Rutgers University Press, 2000), 6–8.

2 See Thomas Leitch, *Film Adaptation and its Discontents: From* Gone with the Wind *to* The Passion of the Christ (Baltimore: Johns Hopkins University Press, 2007), 239.

3 In between these polarities come detective fiction, both traditional and "hard-boiled," espionage novels, and what can broadly be called "mysteries" in the Daphne du Maurier vein. Of course, many crime novels defy these convenient labels and combine elements of two or more categories, and Hitchcock himself seemed to prefer this kind of hybrid: *Strangers on a Train* is hard-boiled but dispenses with the detective favored by Dashiell Hammett and Raymond Chandler; *Rebecca* is both a psychological thriller and a whodunit; *The Lady Vanishes* intertwines a traditional spy plot with a disappearing-woman mystery, and so on. The only subgenre of the crime novel Hitchcock regularly avoided was the traditional Agatha Christie–style murder mystery—he always claimed that suspense is far more interesting than surprise—though elements of the Christie crime puzzles are occasionally included in the mixed-type crime-novel sources Hitchcock preferred (*The Lodger, Murder!, I Confess, Vertigo*)

4 The departures from the norm were generally not well received: *The Trouble with Harry, The Wrong Man.*

5 In addition to being the model for Norman in the novel and film, Gein was the inspiration for several later films, including *The Texas Chainsaw Massacre* (1974) and *The Silence of the Lambs* (1991).

6 Stephen Rebello, *Alfred Hitchcock and the Making of* Psycho (New York: St. Martin's Griffin, 1990).

7 See Paul Anthony Woods, *Ed Gein: Psycho* (New York: St. Martin's Press, 1995).

8 Robert Bloch, *Psycho* (New York: TOR Horror, 1989), 14 (subsequent citations will appear parenthetically in the text).

9 Evan Hunter, *Me and Hitch* (New York: Faber and Faber, 1997), 14; Walter Srebnick, "Working with Hitch: A Screenwriter's Forum with Evan Hunter, Arthur Laurents, and Joseph Stefano," *Hitchcock Annual* (2001–2): 1–37.

10 Daphne du Maurier, "The Birds," in *Classics of the Macabre* (New York: Doubleday, 1987), 154 (subsequent citations will appear parenthetically in the text).

11 Francois Truffaut, *Hitchcock* (New York: Touchstone Books, 1984), 220.

12 Ibid., 218.

13 Qtd. in Tony Lee Moral, *Alfred Hitchcock and the Making of* Marnie (Lanham, Md.: Scarecrow Press, 2002), 7.

14 Winston Graham, *Marnie* (London: Pan Books, 1997), 124 (subsequent citations will appear parenthetically in the text).

CHAPTER 3. FROM TREATMENT TO SCRIPT

1 Budge Crawley, Fletcher Markle, and Gerald Pratley, "I Wish I Didn't Have to Shoot the Picture: An Interview with Alfred Hitchcock," in *Focus on Hitchcock,* ed. Albert J. La Valley (Englewood Cliffs, N.J.: Prentice-Hall, 1972), 26.

2 Ibid., 26–27.

3 Alfred Hitchcock, "Direction" (1937), in *Focus on Hitchcock,* ed. Albert J. La Valley (Englewood Cliffs, N.J.: Prentice-Hall, 1972), 38.

4 Stephen Rebello, *Alfred Hitchcock and the Making of* Psycho (New York: St. Martin's Griffin, 1990), 34–35.

5 Authors' interview with Joseph Stefano, New York City, April 10, 2001.

6 Ibid. Stefano also indicated that there were other revisions of the dialogue tailored to specific actors, but that these were minor.

7 Ibid.

8 Raymond Durgnat, *A Long Hard Look at* Psycho (London: British Film Institute Publishing, 2002), 7.

9 Authors' interview with Hilton Green, Pasadena, California, March 19, 2006.

10 "Dialogue on Film: Alfred Hitchcock," in *Alfred Hitchcock Interviews,* ed. Sidney Gottlieb (Jackson: University Press of Mississippi, 2003), 99.

11 Crawley, Markle, and Pratley, "I Wish I Didn't Have to Shoot the Picture," 24.

12 Stefano interview.

13 Dan Aulier, *Hitchcock's Notebooks* (New York: HarperCollins, 2002), 207.

14 Alfred Hitchcock to Evan Hunter, December 21, 1961, Herrick Library of Motion Picture Arts, Los Angeles.

15 This is evidence that at this stage Hunter was trying to establish a connection between human aggression and the birds.

16 Alfred Hitchcock to Evan Hunter, November 30, 1961, Herrick Library of Motion Picture Arts, Los Angeles.

17 Alfred Hitchcock to V. S. Pritchett, April 9, 1962, Herrick Library of Motion Picture Arts, Los Angeles.

18 V. S. Pritchett to Alfred Hitchcock, April 12, 1962, Herrick Library of Motion Picture Arts, Los Angeles.

19 This is evidence that early on Hunter conceived of Melanie as undergoing a major transformation.

20 Hunter's first draft was not finally pessimistic about the characters'—and human—survival.

21 Francois Truffaut, *Hitchcock* (New York: Touchstone Books, 1984), 288.

22 Ibid.

23 Hitchcock to George R. Isaacs, June 24, 1963, Herrick Library of Motion Picture Arts, Los Angeles.

24 Truffaut, *Hitchcock,* 288.

25 Robert E. Kapsis, *Hitchcock: The Making of a Reputation* (Chicago: University of Chicago Press, 1992), 69–70.

26 Hunter interview. Hunter also said that the audience was confused and silent at the end of the film's premiere.

27 Tony Lee Moral, *Alfred Hitchcock and the Making of* Marnie (Lanham, Md.: Scarecrow Press, 2002), 25.

28 Hunter interview.

29 See Moral, *Alfred Hitchcock and the Making of* Marnie, 26–35.

30 Jay Presson Allen to Alfred Hitchcock, December 16, 1963, Herrick Library of Motion Picture Arts, Los Angeles. Mrs. Edgar's first name was changed several times.

31 Truffaut, *Alfred Hitchcock,* 290.

CHAPTER 4. FINAL DRAFTS: THE SHOOTING SCRIPT

1 David Thomson, *The Moment of* Psycho: *How Alfred Hitchcock Taught America to Love Murder* (New York: Basic Books, 2010), 24.

2 Francois Truffaut, *Hitchcock* (New York: Touchstone Books, 1984), 218.

3 Evan Hunter, *Me and Hitch* (New York: Faber and Faber, 1997), 17–19.

4 Ibid., 21.

5 This is a reading of the text that has been long shared by critics. See, for example, Donald Spoto, *The Art of Alfred Hitchcock* (New York: Doubleday, 1992), 329–38.

6 Authors' interview with Jay Presson Allen, New York City, November 16, 2001.

7 Truffaut, *Hitchcock,* 319.

8 Tony Lee Moral, *Alfred Hitchcock and the Making of* Marnie (Lanham, Md.: Scarecrow Press, 2002), 29.

AFTERWORD

1 Stephen Rebello, *Alfred Hitchcock and the Making of* Psycho (New York: St. Martin's Griffin, 1990), 95.

2 Tony Lee Moral, *Alfred Hitchcock and the Making of* Marnie (Lanham, Md.: Scarecrow Press, 2002), 132–34.

3 Walter Srebnick, "Working with Hitch: A Screenwriter's Forum with Evan Hunter, Arthur Laurents, and Joseph Stefano," *Hitchcock Annual* (2001–2): 17.

4 See Patrick McGilligan, *Alfred Hitchcock: A Life in Darkness and Light* (New York: HarperCollins, 2003), 650–54; Joseph McBride, "Alfred Hitchcock's 'Mary Rose': An Old Master's Unheard Cri de Coeur," *Cineaste* 26.2 (2001): 24–28.

Index

cock, 64–74, 120; dismissed by Hitchcock, 15; favorite Hitchcock film of, 12; final screenplay for *The Birds,* 92–102; Hitchcock's visual style and, 111–12; personality of, xvi; on politics, 21–22; reaction to the final filmed version of *The Birds,* 113, 116–17; selection to work with Hitchcock, 11–16; writing of *Marnie* by, 76–77

Hurley, Joe, 61

Inge, William, 19
intuition, visual, 1, 111–12
Islington Studios, 3

Jung, Carl, 106–7

Kelly, Grace, 7, 14–15, 52
Kennedy, John F., 17–18, 21–22, 23, 69, 98–99, 102, 107
Kinsey Reports, 19
Krohn, Bill, xiii

Laurents, Arthur, 3
Leff, Leonard, 6
Lehman, Ernest, 3, 8, 119
Lifeboat, 6–7
Lloyd, Norman, 6
Lodger, The, 4, 9
Lonely Passion of Judith Hearne, The, 119
Lovecraft, H. P., 27
Lowndes, Marie Belloc, 4

Man Who Knew Too Much, The, xi, 16, 17, 27; source material for, 26
Marnie, 1, 11, 81, 114; Jay Presson Allen script for, 77–80; animal imagery in, 107–10; characterizations in, 103–7; collaboration between Hitchcock and Allen on, 74–80; Evan Hunter script for, 76–77; film differences from the novel, 52–53, 78–79; final screenplay for, 102–12; Grace Kelly and, 14–15; Hitchcock's early visualization of, 14–15; photography in, 80; popularity of, xi; postwar American culture and, 17; protagonist development in, 111–12; psychological exploration in, 19, 105–7; scenes cut from, 104–5; sexuality in, 22–23, 46, 48–49, 51, 102–3; source material for, 26, 45–53; Joseph Stefano script for, 74–75

Mary Rose, 118
masculinity, 23–24
Maslow, Abraham, 18
May, Rollo, 18
McCarthyism, 16
McGilligan, Patrick, 4
Me and Hitch, xvi, 66
melodrama, 94–96
Metalious, Grace, 19
Moore, Brian, 119
Moral, Tony Lee, xiii, 46, 75
My Favorites in Suspense, 15

narrative nature of Hitchcock films, 8–11, 29–34
New York Times, 28, 46
Ngo Din Diem, 17–18
No Bail for the Judge, 26, 27
North by Northwest, 11, 14, 16, 17, 117; *The 39 Steps* and, 26, 27
Notorious, 6, 7, 9, 12, 70

O'Neill, Eugene, 103
Osborne, John, 52
Outer Limits, The, xvi, 15, 114

Paramount, 7
Parker, Dorothy, 3
Perkins, Anthony, 63, 84, 115
Perls, Fritz, 18
Peyton Place, 19
Playhouse 90, xv

politics: liberal, 22, 107; sexual, 18
postwar American culture, 16–24, 21–22, 68–69, 83–84, 98, 102
Prime of Miss Jean Brodie, The, xvii, 13, 119
Prince of the City, xvii, 119
Pritchett, V. S., 70, 117
producers, 6
protagonists, 2, 53–54, 66–68, 111–12
Psycho, xii, 1, 2, 7, 11, 67, 73, 74, 75, 79, 80, 81, 105; Cavanaugh script for, 56–58, 62; characterization of "Mother" in, 85, 90–92; characterizations in, 83–86; collaboration between Hitchcock and Stefano on, 56–64; dialogue in, 59–60, 83, 89–91; film differences from the novel, 31, 35–36; final screenplay for, 82–92; Marion's car in, 88–89; narrative nature of, 29–34; photography in, 59, 60–62; popularity of, xi; postwar American culture and, 16–17, 83–84; protagonist development in, 111–12; psychological exploration in, 11–12, 19–20; sequels, 114–15; sexuality in, 19–20; shower scene, 87–88; social class in, 20–21; source material for, 14, 26, 27–38
psychoanalysis, 11–12, 18–19
Psycho IV: The Beginning, 115

Quine, Richard, xvi

Rear Window, xi, 2, 7, 11, 17; source material for, 25, 26
Rebecca, 6, 9, 11, 12
Rebello, Stephen, xiii, 58
Reville, Alma, 4, 6, 12, 114, 118
Robertson, Peggy, 114
Rogers, Carl, 18
Rohmer, Eric, xviii

romantic comedy, 92–94
Rope, xi, xii

Schmenner, Will, xiii
screwball comedies, 92–94
Selznick, David O., 6, 25, 81
sexuality in American culture: portrayed in *Marnie,* 22–23, 46, 48–49, 51, 102–3; portrayed in *Psycho,* 19–20
sexual politics, 18
Shadow of a Doubt, 6, 9, 11, 70
Shaffer, Anthony, 119
Short stories, films as, 3–4, 8
Silitoe, Allan, 52
Sirk, Douglas, 19
Sleuth, 119
social class, 20–21, 75
source material used by Hitchcock, 4–6, 7, 14; for *The Birds,* 38–45; intensity of, 26–27; for *Marnie,* 45–53; for *Psycho,* 27–38; rewritten, 7, 27; types of preferred, 25–26. See also *Birds, The; Marnie; Psycho*
Spellbound, 6, 7
Spoto, Donald, xv
Stannard, Eliot, 3, 4
Stefano, Joseph, 2, 70, 80; characterizations by, 83–86; collaboration with Hitchcock, 58–64, 119–20; favorite Hitchcock film of, 12; final screenplay for *Psycho,* 82–92; Hitchcock's visual style and, 111–12; other writing projects of, xv–xvi, 113–14; personality of, xv; psychological knowledge of, 13; reaction to the final filmed version of *Psycho,* 113–14; selection to work with Hitchcock, 11–16; sexual references used by, 19–20; work in later years, 115; writing of *Marnie* by, 74–75
Steinbeck, John, 6
Stewart, James, 7

WALTER RAUBICHECK
is a professor of English at
Pace University and the coeditor
of *Going My Way: Bing Crosby
and American Culture.*

WALTER SREBNICK
is Professor Emeritus of English
at Pace University and the coeditor
of *Hitchcock's Rereleased Films:
From* Rope *to* Vertigo.

The University of Illinois Press
is a founding member of the
Association of American University Presses.

University of Illinois Press
1325 South Oak Street
Champaign, IL 61820-6903
www.press.uillinois.edu